THE RESPONSE OF THE CHURCH
IN CHANGING JAPAN

The

RESPONSE of the CHURCH
in CHANGING JAPAN

edited by

CHARLES H. GERMANY

FRIENDSHIP PRESS
New York

CONTENTS

INTRODUCTION

The Response of the Church in Changing Japan focuses attention on two significant aspects of Japanese life today. The rapidity of change in major areas of life—family, neighborhood, school, factory, farm, city, law, politics, international relations—is almost breathtaking, as breathtaking as the new high-speed trains that travel over 100 miles per hour along the eastern seaboard. The change, furthermore, is not only rapid but sufficiently deep to call attention to a new age in Japan. More than this, the new age exists in a growing atmosphere of world awareness.

At the same time, the new age has not blotted out the "old Japan." True, it is not yet clear how Japan's national heritage will finally express itself within the currents of contemporary life. To suppose, however, that this heritage has been shunted aside by advanced modernization and internationalism would be superficial indeed. A helpful perspective on Japan today, therefore, will contain the awareness of two focuses of concern in national life—the achievement of a new international role and a new understanding of the nature of Japan's inner identity.

The presence of two such concerns and the struggle to keep them in balance are not new in Japan's history. The two forces were active in the 1860's when Japan was reopened after 250 years of isolation. At that time a host of world influences poured into "Meiji" Japan—new education, new industry, new laws and new government. Some Japanese capitulated temporarily to the new world influences. Others retreated into a hardened feudal nationalism. Most tried to relate the new and the old, the outer and the inner, in such a way as to find meaning for personal life and for the nation.

Protestant Christianity was among the new influences that flowed into Japan in the new age. Kanzō Uchimura illustrates as clearly as any figure of that time the effort to relate creatively the new and the old. Uchimura wrote:

A Japanese by becoming a Christian does not cease to be a Japanese. On the contrary, he becomes more Japanese by becoming a Christian. A Japanese who becomes an American or an Englishman, or an amorphous universal man, is neither a true Japanese nor a true Christian. Paul, a Christian apostle, remained an Hebrew of the Hebrews till the end of his life. Savonarola was an Italian Christian, Luther was a German Christian, and Knox was a Scotch Christian. They were not characterless universal men, but distinctly national, therefore distinctly human and distinctly Christian. . . .

I have seen no more sorrowful figures than Japanese who imitate their American or European missionary-teachers by being converted to the faith of the latter. Closely examined, these converted "universal Christians" may turn out to be no more than denationalized Japanese, whose universality is no more than Americanism or Anglicanism adopted to cover up their lost nationality.[1]

[1] Footnotes begin on page 170.

There follows Uchimura's well-known passage on the "two J's":

I love two J's and no third; one is Jesus, and other is Japan.
I do not know which I love more, Jesus or Japan.
I am hated by my countrymen for Jesus' sake as *yaso*, and I am disliked by foreign missionaries for Japan's sake as national and narrow.
No matter; I may lose all my friends, but I cannot lose Jesus and Japan.[2]

The adjustment of the national or personal and a strong international influence with which Uchimura struggled is the adjustment that Japan today is seeking to make in relation to the world outside her and the change within.

Moreover, it is against this background of searching and adjustment in national life that the Christian church in Japan today will be set forth in this study. Within the life of the church, also, we see the new age and the old Japan. Chapter 5 will describe the contemporary international involvement of the church, but the attendant concern is simultaneously present—the struggle to define the true inner selfhood of the church.

"My faith," Uchimura wrote, "is not a circle with one center; it is an ellipse with two centers." [3] The ellipse with the two centers describes the spirit and character of most nations and churches throughout the world, and not least that of Japan and the Japanese church.

The account that follows begins with a historical sketch of the past century in Japan, told by James Phillips through the life story of three great Christian leaders. The review of the contemporary social, political and cultural scene by

David Swain in Chapter 2 is set against the background of a drama written by a Japanese playwright in the days following Japan's defeat in World War II. The choices before the nation today, Mr. Swain feels, are similar to those confronting Japan in the turbulent latter half of the nineteenth century. A description of the Christian community in Japan today is presented by Yoichiro Saeki in Chapter 3. Chapter 4 lifts up, out of the total contemporary life and work of the church, a few of the ministries that seem particularly relevant to the crucial challenges in national life. The book closes with a picture of the inspiring growth in world responsibility on the part of a Japanese church that has known in the depths of its own life the grace of forgiveness, renewal, and the act of reconciliation.

CHARLES H. GERMANY

1

TODAY'S LEGACY FROM
YESTERDAY'S LEADERS

JAMES M. PHILLIPS

The Christian church in Japan owes much to the pioneers of the past, both those who lived and worked in the years when Christianity first gained a toehold in Japan and those who belong to the more recent past. In this chapter, the lives of three men—an educator and a pastor of the nineteenth century and a prophetic social reformer of the twentieth—offer concrete examples of "today's legacy from yesterday's leaders."

Jō Niijima: Educator

A COURAGEOUS EXIT

In the spring of 1864, a small Japanese boat set sail from the harbor of Edo, the future Tokyo, which was at that time the governmental seat of the Shōgun, or military dictator. The ship was headed for Hakodate on Japan's northern island of Hokkaidō, one of the two ports that had recently been opened by treaty for American shipping. Aboard was

11

a young Japanese of the samurai or warrior class, named Shimeta Niijima, who cherished a secret resolve in his heart. His family, who had seen him off in Edo, assumed that he was simply following the command of his feudal master to go to Hakodate and continue his studies of Western learning. But young Niijima had something else in mind. He had resolved to take the first chance he could to smuggle himself aboard a ship bound for the United States, to pursue Western learning on its own shores. In doing so Niijima would be taking a desperate chance, for it was a capital offense for any Japanese to go abroad without permission. But to the mind of this energetic twenty-one-year-old youth, the times were desperate and they cried out for desperate remedies.

Only eleven years before, a convoy of black ships had sailed into that same Edo Bay, under the command of Commodore Matthew Perry from the United States. The efforts of that commander had forced the Shōgun the following year to sign a treaty that ended Japan's self-imposed policy of isolation, which had been in effect for more than two centuries. Perry's visit had started a chain reaction of events within Japan. Many Japanese, especially those in the more restive clans in western Japan, denounced the feeble, temporizing efforts of the Shōgun's government to come to terms with the foreigners. They adopted as their slogan, "Honor the Emperor, expel the Barbarians!" Honoring the Emperor they certainly could do, but expelling the barbarians was more easily said than done.

Foreigners had established regular contact with Japan with the arrival of St. Francis Xavier in 1549, after which missionaries and traders from Spain and Portugal came to Japan in considerable numbers. At the very time when European Christendom was locked in the struggles resulting from the Protestant Reformation, a relatively small group of missionaries, mostly from the Jesuit order, were winning large numbers of Japanese to Christianity. By 1614 there may have been as many as 300,000 Roman Catholic Christians in Japan, or about one and one-half percent of the total population. But for a variety of reasons, political and social as well as religious, the government set about to exterminate the Christian community and expel its foreign priests. Thereafter the Shōgunate policy was to limit contacts with foreigners to a small group of Dutch traders, who were restricted to an island in Nagasaki harbor.

An interesting fact of Japanese Christian history is that the early Roman Catholic community was never entirely exterminated. Although the forms of the faith became somewhat distorted over the centuries because of absence of leadership and isolation, a minority of believers persisted into modern times in handing on the Christian faith received through St. Francis Xavier.

In the nineteenth century, it was evident to most thoughtful Japanese that it would not be as easy to "expel the barbarians" as it had been in the seventeenth. The power of Western nations was growing, and spheres of influence had already been carved out by European nations throughout Africa and Asia. Particularly disturbing in Japan were the encroachments that European powers were making on her great neighbor China, from whom had come her cultural heritage, her system of writing and her chief instruction in the Buddhist faith. Now the young nation, the United States, was taking the lead in opening Japan to foreign trade and influence after the long period of isolation, and other nations were to follow in its wake. Japan realized that she had to come to terms with these powerful foreigners, but how was she best to do it?

For a few Japanese like Niijima, the Westerners and their learning were a source of great fascination. Through Chinese translations of Western books that had been smuggled into the country, they had developed a great curiosity about the West. Some of the ideas of the Western religion called Christianity intrigued Niijima as he read about them secretly. Here too he was venturing along dangerous paths, for in the public places throughout Japan there stood edict boards threatening death to any of the followers of the religion of Jesus. But undeterred by the dangers, Niijima succeeded in escaping from Hakodate as a stowaway on a ship going to Shanghai, from whence he took another ship to America, which for him was the land of promise.

ARRIVAL OF THE EARLY MISSIONARIES

Even before Niijima's escape, the barriers between Japan and the outside world had started to come down. As a result of the treaties America had signed with the Shōgun's government, American missionaries had started arriving in Japan to make preparations for spreading the Christian faith as soon as opportunity permitted. In 1859 had come the first Protestant missionaries: the Rev. John Liggins and the Rev. C. M. Williams of the Episcopal Church; the Rev. and Mrs. S. R. Brown, Dr. and Mrs. D. B. Simmons and the

Rev. and Mrs. Guido F. Verbeck of the Reformed Church; and Dr. and Mrs. James C. Hepburn of the Presbyterian Church. They were joined in the following year by the Rev. and Mrs. Jonathan Goble of the Baptist Church, in 1861 by Dr. and Mrs. James Ballagh of the Reformed Church and in 1863 by the Rev. and Mrs. David Thompson of the Presbyterian Church. The outbreak of the American Civil War prevented the sending of more missionaries until 1869, when the first missionary of the American Board arrived.

The year 1873 reflected a new surge of interest in Japan on the part of Western churches. The debilitating war between the states had ended. The Iwakura mission had aroused concern for Japan; and in this year twenty-nine missionaries joined the early arrivals. Now the Methodist Episcopal Church, the American Baptist Churches and the Canadian Methodist Church were involved in Christian work in Japan. Other workers arrived from Great Britain, and during the decade of the 1870's the Evangelical Association, the German Reformed Church and the Methodist Protestant Church established missions in Japan. A great range of evangelistic educational and social work developed, and medical work grew.

The names of the pioneer missionaries and those who joined them are written large in Japanese history, not only in church work but also in linguistic studies, medicine, education, government service and social welfare. Despite denominational differences, most of the early missionaries had been deeply influenced by the ethos of American Puritanism. This ethos was to have a great attraction for Japanese of samurai background like Niijima, who had been brought up on Confucian ethics which bore many resemblances to those of Puritanism. To some of the Japanese who formed their "bands" (even the use of the English word "band" reveals a kinship with Puritan covenant ethics) under the inspiration of the foreign missionaries it seemed that loyalty to Christ might represent the fulfilment of the highest ideals of Confucian ethics and of *Bushidō*, the code of the samurai.

EDUCATION IN THE UNITED STATES

Not long after he arrived in the United States in 1865, Niijima began to receive a Puritan-style education under the patronage of the owner of the ship on which he had sailed to America, Alpheus Hardy. In gratitude to Hardy for his help, Niijima came to style himself in English "Joseph Hardy Neeshima." He was graduated from the Phillips Academy in Andover, Massachusetts, and then received his BS at Amherst College. His interest in Christianity had led him during his voyage to America to sell his short samurai sword in order to buy a Chinese New Testament. His Christian faith grew deeper during his stay in America, and he was baptized while he was at Phillips Academy. After college he decided to prepare himself for the Christian ministry by returning to Andover to enter the theological seminary. While he was there, his studies were interrupted by a request from an important delegation that was sent abroad from his home country.

Back in Japan drastic changes had been taking place after the Meiji Restoration. Members of discontented clans in western Japan had succeeded in bringing about the collapse of the Shōgunate in 1867 and the theoretical restoration of the Emperor to full governmental power. The new group of men who advised the young Meiji Emperor became convinced that instead of seeking to "expel the barbarians," the best way for Japan to achieve equality with Western nations was to adopt Western ways as quickly and as thoroughly as possible. The Emperor promised in his Charter Oath of 1868 that "Knowledge shall be sought throughout the world so as to strengthen the foundations of imperial rule."

One consequence of this policy was that a mission was sent abroad under Count Iwakura to seek revision of the unequal treaties with foreign nations and to make studies for a new educational system for Japan. It was this mission that requested Niijima in 1872 to join it as an interpreter, promising that in return he would be completely absolved of his breach of the law in leaving the country. After some hesitation Niijima accepted the invitation and joined the mission for eighteen months on a tour of America and Europe.

On tour the Iwakura mission found that one reason Western nations professed unwillingness to amend the unequal treaties was the Japanese government's suppression of Christianity. Hence the mission urged that the edict boards banning Christianity be removed, and this was done in 1873. The observations that the mission made of educational institutions proved extremely valuable in the development of the Japanese educational system. As a result of the trip, Niijima came to attach great importance to the need for founding a Christian institution of higher education that would help to guide the nation's future course.

After completing his work with the Iwakura mission, Niijima returned to Andover to finish his theological course and was ordained to the ministry. He was then appointed a corresponding member of the Japan mission of the American Board of Commissioners for Foreign Missions, serving the Congregational Churches, and to them he broached his plan for a Christian college for Japan. The board members gave little support to his plan, for they were understandably reluctant to take on the added responsibility of a new school when their budget was already allocated. Undaunted, Niijima waited for his turn to address the annual meeting of the board, and ended an emotional appeal for his school with these words: "I cannot go back to Japan without the money to found a Christian college, and I am going to stand here until I get it." It is said that within a few minutes, nearly five thousand dollars were promised on the spot!

RETURN TO JAPAN

The Japan to which Niijima returned in 1874 was in the midst of full-scale efforts to strengthen and modernize the country by what was surely one of the most peaceful, yet thoroughgoing, social revolutions in history. To this day the developing nations of Asia and Africa have been attempting with varying degrees of success to duplicate the "Meiji miracle." Niijima found that the Emperor's residence had been moved from Kyoto to his own city of Edo, now renamed Tokyo and made the national capital. The government was trying to modernize Japan at an accelerated rate, by official sponsorship of Western-type governmental agencies, military establishments, industrial enterprises, schools and universities, even dance halls. Though generally in support of the goals to which all this ferment was leading,

Niijima and his friends were disturbed by the attitude of the Meiji government toward religion. At first the government set out to create a state cult of Shintō, Japan's native animistic faith. In order to do this the government tried to bring to an end the system of "Double Aspect" Shintō whereby, centuries before, Shintō had been virtually amalgamated with a number of beliefs and practices of Buddhism.

Buddhism had been introduced from Korea in the sixth century and had become more thoroughly indigenized in the thirteenth century under the guidance of Japanese spiritual leaders. But because Buddhist groups had allowed themselves over the years to be used by the now-defunct Tokugawa Shōgunate, the new Meiji rulers hoped to establish Shintō as the symbolic center in which the sentiment of the empire would be focused. The weakness of the Shintō groups themselves, however, together with the resurgence of the Buddhist sects which saw their position threatened by both Shintō and Christianity, led the Meiji government to allow a measure of freedom to all three religious groups.

Here Niijima saw his great opportunity. He would found his Christian college to provide spiritual orientation for his rapidly developing country. At length he established his school, the Dōshisha—literally "the common-purpose association"—on land just north of the former Imperial Palace in Kyoto, where by its very location it would witness to Christianity's presence at the heart of the nation's traditional life.

Niijima opened the doors of the Dōshisha in 1875 to a handful of mediocre students. His hopes might have floundered at the outset had not the school been strengthened by the transfer from the Kumamoto School of Western Learning of the Kumamoto Band, an earnest and intelligent company of students who had become ardent Christians under the leadership of their American teacher, Captain L. L. Janes. The remaining years of Niijima's life were given over to strengthening the Dōshisha and the young Christian congregations in Japan.

DIFFICULTIES THEN AND NOW

Some of the patterns and problems with which Niijima dealt have continued ever since. One of these was the development of a close relationship between Christian schools like Dōshisha and the local church congregations that were subsequently established. The schools, by means of strong Christian leadership, led in the establishment of churches, including in most cases continuing contributions to the financial support of the churches. This pattern is virtually the reverse of the pattern of frontier America, where the churches were instrumental in the founding of Christian schools. One result is that the churches have won from among the thousands of graduates of the Christian schools a great many sympathizers and a substantial number of converts.

Another problem encountered by Japanese Christian schools from Niijima's day to the present is that of obtaining adequate financial resources. Christian schools have found themselves in competition with other private or government-run schools, which have been able to call on more resources and thus to attract better faculty and students. Christian schools have had to struggle with the ordeals of meeting rising costs and finding competent faculty members, while still maintaining their Christian purpose.

Niijima was also concerned with the problem of how best to utilize the services of Western missionaries in an independent Japanese institution, and this problem has grown as the Japanese Christian schools and churches have become increasingly able to stand on their own feet. Some Japanese felt that the missionaries' very presence was an affront to Japanese national pride, while others were eager to receive aid of whatever kind was offered, on the missionaries' own terms. Niijima tried to mediate between these two positions, a task that has also been a continuing responsibility for Japanese Christian leaders.

Still another problem, which was to engage Niijima in the final year of his life, was that of Japanese church unity. He opposed a plan to unite the Congregational Churches, with which he was affiliated, with the Church of Christ in Japan, which had been started under Presbyterian and Reformed auspices. Largely because of his opposition, the plan was defeated. But the problem remained: How could Japanese Christians witness to their unity in Christ in a form that was not merely an echo of the experiences of Christians in other lands and other times?

DECLINING YEARS

Despite such problems, the closing years of Niijima's life saw Christianity riding a great wave of popularity in Japan, and it was even suggested that Japan might become predominantly Christian by 1900. Some Japanese who had no personal interest in Christianity nevertheless thought that it might be in the nation's interest to become Christian in order to be more easily accepted as an equal by Western nations. In such a climate, Christian schools grew in number and in strength, and church membership increased almost four times within a few years. Yet this very growth brought new problems, for some people embraced Christianity not for its own sake but simply as a means of becoming Westernized or gaining social status. As a result, Japanese churches often became stereotyped as urban, middle-class enclaves, and strenuous efforts have often been required to remake such a public image.

Niijima died in 1890, not long before his forty-seventh birthday. He will always be remembered primarily as an educator, and thus revered not only by the Christian community but also by the public at large. Indeed his very role as the founder of a great educational institution gave him a niche in Japanese history that has tended to obscure for many people the Christian purpose that underlay all he did. Beyond doubt, the slight and peppery Japanese youth who set sail from Edo Harbor on a spring day in 1864 would call all men to remember that truly great institutions draw greatness from the faith that gives them life.

Masahisa Uemura: Pastor

THE EARLY CHURCHMAN

In the last year of his life Niijima had, out of his sense of loyalty to Alpheus Hardy and the Congregational Churches in the United States, kept the Congregational Churches from participating in the newly organized Church of Christ in Japan (which was to be the largest Protestant body in the nation). One of the principal organizers of the United Church was Masahisa Uemura, who by that time had already achieved considerable stature as a Christian leader. A member of the Yokohama Band, who had received his education under the guidance of Dr. Ballagh and Dr. Brown, Uemura had been one of the early members of the first Protestant church in Japan, the *Nihon Kirisuto Kōkai*, "The Japan Christian Public Association," founded in 1872 with Dr. Ballagh as pastor. The founders had purposely refrained from giving this first church a denominational label because of their conviction that Japanese Christianity needed to find its own expression outside the denominational categories of Western Christendom.

Uemura's dominant concern from the start had been the proper guidance and strengthening of church life. He became a member of the committee that translated the Old Testament into Japanese, along with a number of hymns that appeared in a hymnal in 1903 and have been used ever since.

Uemura was untiring in his efforts to found and to strengthen local churches. His evangelistic work in the central Tokyo area led to the establishment of the Shitaya Itchi Church in 1879. This became the Fujimichō Church, and it was for many years the largest Protestant congregation in Japan. He served this church as pastor to the end of his life, but he also gave encouragement and assistance to the founding of other local churches, particularly in the Tokyo area. Although not primarily an educator like Niijima, he sought to strengthen theological education and to develop it along lines suited to the particular needs of Japan. When a dispute arose in the theological department of Meiji Gakuin, where Uemura was a professor of theology, he withdrew and with some colleagues founded the Tokyo Theological Seminary. This was the first independent theological school in Japan, and one of the main predecessors of the present Tokyo Union Theological Seminary.

ENCOUNTER WITH UCHIMURA

In addition to his organizational abilities, Uemura is also remembered for the significant battles he waged as a Christian apologist. In 1891 the attention of the whole nation was attracted by an incident that involved Kanzō Uchimura. Uchimura had been a member of the independent-minded Sapporo Band, which had been organized at the Agricultural College in Sapporo under the lay leadership of Dr. William S. Clark. Clark's Puritan discipline together with his fatherly concern for his pupils and his constant encouragement of study of the Scriptures left its impact on his charges, even as his departing words to his pupils have become something of a legend in Japan: "Boys, be ambitious!"

After his graduation from the Sapporo Agricultural College, Uchimura was appointed a history instructor at the prestigious First Higher School in Tokyo. As a reaction in part to the craze for Westernization in the 1880's, the government had taken measures to strengthen Japanese nationalism. The promulgation of the Meiji Constitution in 1889 had granted Japanese subjects "freedom of religious belief," but had hedged this right by keeping it "within limits not prejudicial to peace and order, and not antagonistic to their duties as subjects." The specific content of these limitations was made clear the following year in the Imperial Rescript on Education, which concluded with the Shintō-laden exhortation, ". . . should emergency arise, offer yourselves courageously to the State, and thus guard and maintain the prosperity of Our Imperial Throne, coeval with heaven and earth." A copy of the Imperial Rescript on Education and portraits of the Emperor and Empress were installed in all schools, and students and faculty members were required to bow before them. At the First Higher School, when Uchimura's turn came to bow, he acted on a sudden impulse and stood erect before the documents. It seemed to him as a Christian that such a bow would mean worshiping an inanimate object.

In the furor that ensued over this incident, the basic issues were soon overlooked, as was the fact that Uchimura from his sickbed subsequently retracted his original position and sent a representative to bow on his behalf. A hue and cry arose among Japanese critics of Christianity that it was impossible for a Christian to be a loyal subject of the emperor. Masahisa Uemura fearlessly printed a defense of Uchimura's original action in his *Fukuin Shūhō* (*The Gospel Weekly*), but as a result of this article the authorities forced the periodical to suspend publication. The intrepid Uemura was soon in print again with a new periodical that had only a slightly different name, *Fukuin Shimpō* (*The Gospel News*).

Although the friendship between Uchimura and Uemura continued, their views on the nature of the church soon diverged sharply. Both were concerned that Japanese Christianity achieve a strong basis of self-support and self-propagation, and hence both stressed that Japanese Christians should not allow themselves to become spiritually or financially subservient to foreign mission boards or missionaries. But Uchimura followed this up by insisting that Japanese Christianity must also reject the very organizational form of the church in order to enable Christians to concentrate on Bible study, prayer and Christian witness. The *Mukyōkai* ("Non-Church") movement which Uchimura founded has enjoyed considerable success down to the present, although its very lack of organizational structure and continuity has proved to be its main weakness as well as its main strength. For his part, Uemura stoutly rejected Uchimura's disdain for the organized church, characterized, Uchimura felt, by inessential denominational differences. To Uemura, the visible church was the model of the invisible church of God.

ENCOUNTER WITH EBINA

Uemura also took issue with fellow Christians who, he believed, had fallen too much under the influence of the "New Theology," introduced by Unitarians and others in the late 1880's. Such persons were eager to reject the church's doctrinal developments, particularly in regard to Christology. After Tsūrin Kanamori published a work in which he repudiated the traditional affirmations of Christ's deity, Uemura countered by maintaining that Christians needed to confess the divine nature of Christ or else surrender the claim that faith in Christ means a relationship with the living God. A few years later Uemura took up the question of Christology again with his friend and fellow Tokyo pastor, Danjō Ebina, in a series of magazine articles. Taking his stand on the

Christological affirmations that had been hammered out at the time of the Council of Chalcedon, Uemura contended that to give up belief in Christ's deity meant to relegate Christianity to a cultural expression of human wisdom about God, rather than a revelation of the Word of God himself, made flesh in Jesus Christ.

Doubtless the significance of these Christological debates was lost on many, but for Uemura they were far removed from theological hair-splitting. He feared that under the pressures of nationalism and cultural conformity, Japanese Christians were being tempted to dilute the content of their faith in Christ, and that it had become simply one more cultural expression of religious truth along with others. If so, the way would be open for the complete disintegration of Christian faith under the acids of skepticism and relativism. Uemura's fears were well founded, for as the spirit of nationalism grew stronger throughout the country, numbers of Christians left the church. In fact, the phenomenon of "graduated Christians" has continued to be a problem for the Japanese churches, as many baptized people have gradually dropped their interest in the church and have at length given up the Christian faith altogether. Yet Uemura's emphasis on orthodox doctrine had its pitfalls, too, for at times some of his followers have tended to place such a strong emphasis on purity of doctrine that the fruits of the Christian faith—in personal experience and in social action—have been neglected.

The period of testing and trials into which the Japanese Christian community was moving brought with it a new approach to biblical faith. Just as Niijima had been concerned with establishing strong bases for Christian evangelism in the schools and churches, Uemura's aim was to strengthen the churches so that they might keep the Christian faith intact in spite of society's pressures to the contrary. One might say that the scriptural focus of Japanese Christianity was shifting from the gospels and the book of Acts, where it had been in the early part of the Meiji era, to the Pauline Epistles, particularly the Epistle to the Romans. The earlier period was characterized by concern for the strength of character shown by Christ's life and death and by the perseverance of the apostles in founding churches. The later period was concerned with the problems of maintaining the integrity of the faith in the church in the midst of the perils and trials of the world.

THE PASTORAL GIFT

The measure of Uemura must be taken in somewhat different fashion from that of Niijima. For although Uemura too was an educator, his role in the church was primarily that of a pastor. He helped to give a particular Japanese flavor to his role as pastor, not only as a shepherd of a local congregation but also as a spiritual teacher, a leader in theological education and an overseer and counselor for the denomination as a whole. For such a pastor, no local or personal problem was too insignificant, nor was any challenge from outside the church too formidable to engage his concern. Under his guidance, local congregations met faithfully each week to hear a thorough exposition of the Scriptures, which would strengthen the doctrinal bases of their faith. Such churches might at times appear to be self-centered spiritual citadels of pious middle-class people struggling to maintain the purity of their faith amid the swirling social ferment around them. But at their best, Japanese local churches have been what a pastor like Uemura intended them to be—centers for scriptural study and fellowship among people who endeavor to be active witnesses to Christ in their society.

Uemura himself spared no efforts on behalf of his congregations. When in September 1923 vast areas of Tokyo and Yokohama were reduced to ruins by an earthquake and subsequent fires, causing an estimated 200,000 deaths and more than a billion dollars in property damages, Uemura spent the last years of his life in helping care for the victims and in enabling groups like his own Fujimichō congregation to rebuild their sanctuaries. When he died in 1925, many churches around the nation and throughout the Empire had special reason to express gratitude for his great life and ministry.

Toyohiko Kagawa: Prophet

EARLY SOCIAL CONCERN

The same earthquake that engaged the efforts of the aging Uemura was instrumental in bringing to Tokyo another pastor, Toyohiko Kagawa, who had already become quite well known for his work among the slum dwellers in Kobe.

Although he came from the same general church background as Uemura, Kagawa was a different kind of person altogether. The story about how he as a seminary student had moved into Kobe's Shinkawa slum district to live among the people there, and the account of this experience in his autobiographical novel *Across the Death Line* (given the English title *Before the Dawn*), made him widely known throughout Japan and overseas as well. After completing his BD at Princeton Theological Seminary he returned to Kobe and, with the assistance of his devoted wife, threw himself into the crucial social problems of that area. In so doing he was by no means unique among Christians, but it was an extremely unusual step for an ordained minister. During the Meiji era, Christians had pioneered in social work. When the Japanese government was asked in 1956 to name the four outstanding Japanese social workers, the list read as follows: Jūji Ishii, founder of the Okayama Orphanage; Kōsuke Tomeoka, who worked in prison reform; Gumpei Yamamuro, who helped to establish the Salvation Army in Japan and took part in numerous social projects; and Takeō Iwahashi, founder of the Light House for the Blind in Osaka. All four were active Christian laymen!

Despite these promising beginnings, Japanese Christians came to have less and less interest in those who were at the bottom of society. It was this situation that Kagawa sought to redress. He encouraged the establishment of labor unions in Japan and accepted posts of responsibility in these unions long before the labor movement had achieved respectability. When labor trouble broke out in the Kobe area, Kagawa plunged into the midst of it, working toward a settlement by championing what he felt were the just rights of the workers. He also became concerned for the plight of the nation's farmers who worked under unrelenting pressures of tenantry and debt. In 1921 he organized the Japan National Farmers' Union. About the same time he was also instrumental in organizing the first consumers' cooperative in Japan, and in promoting the cooperative movement in general. All this experience lay behind Kagawa when he hastened to Tokyo to assist in relief distribution and rehabilitation after the great 1923 earthquake. He was prevailed upon to stay, and from then on Tokyo was the base of his operations.

THE LIBERAL ERA

The 1920's were active and fruitful days for the liberal movement in Japan. The growth of Japan's economy led to increasing centralization of industrial power in the hands of the *zaibatsu*, or industrial combines, but it also resulted in the emergence of labor unions and political parties, which had widespread popular support. It was Kagawa's hope that the Socialist movement in Japan could be channeled into constructive courses, and he used all his powers of persuasion in speaking and writing to give meaningful help to the Socialist movement. But increasingly the movement inclined toward communism, unlike the Socialist movements of Europe, which Kagawa admired and regarded as constructive alternatives to communism. He was deeply bewildered by the churches' lack of concern for the laboring and farming classes, both of which had hardly been touched by Christian evangelism. To reach them he initiated an evangelistic campaign in 1925, with the goal of making one million converts to Christianity. In 1930 he also started the Kingdom of God Movement, to reach groups that had until then been almost unevangelized. Although both movements fell short of their numerical goals, they helped stir the churches out of some of their complacency about their evangelistic responsibilities.

RISE OF NATIONALISM

The 1930's saw the collapse of much of the liberalism of the previous decade and the rise to power of Japanese militarism. Since 1895, Japan had gone to war about every ten years; and the nation had always been on the winning side, in wars that apparently helped to increase her national power and wealth. It is easy to see how some could conclude that engaging in war was sure to be a very profitable business. During the 1920's the ultraconservative nationalists in Japan became deeply disturbed at the "dangerous thoughts" unleashed by the liberal epoch and at the country's seemingly inevitable drift toward bolshevism. The Mukden Incident in 1931, which led to the Japanese seizure of Manchuria, was a turning point. After this the militarists had their way in Japanese national affairs until the end of World War II.

Apart from a few outspoken pacifists like Kanzō Uchimura, most Japanese Christians had given their approval to the expansion of their country's political power and to its military exploits, or had at least remained silent. In the 1920's, however, the pacifist sentiments which were so widespread elsewhere during the disillusionment following World War I spread to Japan. Kagawa had long been a pacifist by conviction, and he had made world peace one of the primary objectives of the Friends of Jesus group that he had founded in 1921. His writings continued to attack the armament industry and to espouse the pacifist position. In 1928 he founded the National Anti-War League. As the tempo of the militarists' activities increased in the 1930's, his opposition to war grew accordingly, a fact that brought him increasingly under the grave displeasure of the Japanese government.

CHURCHES IN THE VALLEY OF DARKNESS

As it turned out, there was little that a pacifist like Kagawa could do to forestall the coming of Pearl Harbor, despite his earnest attempts at mediation between America and Japan. Other Christian leaders, with Kagawa, were seeking to express concern for reconciliation and fellowship up to the very eve of the outbreak of the war. Japan entered what her writers have called a *kurai tanima*, a "dark valley," from which she was to emerge only after the American battleship *Missouri* sailed into the same Tokyo Bay that Commodore Perry's ships had entered and from which Niijima's ship had sailed. There in 1945 the armistice was signed that brought history's greatest conflict to a close.

Japan's churches suffered a great deal in that "dark valley." Government pressure succeeded in bringing about in June 1941 what the efforts of churchmen themselves had not yet been able to achieve, the formation of the *Nihon Kirisuto Kyōdan*, the United Church of Christ in Japan. But the very pressure which the government and society as a whole had exerted, and which church leaders themselves came to accept, meant that some groups had been forced into the Kyōdan against their will. Hence after the war, the Anglican and Lutheran Churches, as well as a portion of the Presbyterian, Holiness and Baptist groups, left the Kyōdan and have continued their own denominational life. For the majority of the Kyōdan's members, however—who comprise about half of Japan's Protestant community—church union between Methodists, Congregationalists, Reformed believers, Evangelical United Brethren believers, Disciples, members of United Church of Canada background and most Presbyterians, together with some Baptists and Holiness groups, was to be a permanent fact of church life.

POSTWAR RENEWAL

The scene that greeted Kagawa and his fellow Christian leaders after the war was to prove both hopeful and discouraging for the Christian cause. At first large numbers of Japanese flocked into the churches in order to learn more about what they supposed was the religion of their nation's conquerors. Christian schools made an earlier institutional recovery than did the churches and were able to welcome back to Japan large numbers of missionaries, predominantly from Canada and the United States. Missionaries who came to work under the Kyōdan's auspices consolidated their efforts through the Interboard Committee for Christian Work in Japan, and joint committees of Japanese and missionaries were created to establish new patterns of cooperation to reflect the new realities of the church situation. Church membership nearly doubled in the postwar era. A large number of independent missions began work in Japan and undertook programs of Christian outreach, largely in areas untouched by the older groups. Among numerous new institutions that were founded in the postwar era, International Christian University is an outstanding example of a cooperative and creative venture in Christian higher education.

Yet the years since 1945 have seen their share of problems for the Christian cause also, and Kagawa's prophetic eye was one of the first to discern these problems. In their very concern for institutional reconstruction, the churches at times seemed to be turning their backs on the new, highly industrialized society that was growing up around them. To be sure, there were committees formed for meeting various problems, but committees have always proved to be a poor substitute for life. A postwar spiritual vacuum came about after the collapse of the older nationalism and its religious expressions. This vacuum was filled not to any large extent by the Christian churches, but rather by Marxism functioning as a pseudo-religion and by the "new religions." These latter groups are syncretistic, combining elements of Japan's traditional Shintō and Buddhist faiths with newer components.

When Japan's Protestant Centennial celebrations were held in Tokyo in 1959, Toyohiko Kagawa was invited to give an address at one of the evening programs. By then, however, he was confined to his sickbed—he was to die the following year. Hence the assembly heard a tape recording of a message made at his bedside. The thin, frail voice they heard was that of a man who represented some of the finest traditions of Japanese Christian leadership. Like Niijima, he had been an educator and a founder of institutions. But some of the institutions he began have barely managed to survive, while others have developed strength under leadership that has not been predominantly Christian. Like Uemura, he was a lifelong pastor and reached thousands in all walks of life with the Christian message. Yet he was never asked to hold an important post of responsibility within his own denomination, and most of his Christian projects were carried on quite independently of the established churches. Kagawa's true measure may be taken as a prophet, and as such his kind has been scarce indeed in Japan. He felt a prophetic call to turn the attention of the Christian community toward the unreached masses of people in the population at large, and to turn the attention of society as a whole to the unresolved problems of economic cooperation and human brotherhood in the service of peace.

KAGAWA IN RETROSPECT

If Kagawa must be understood primarily as a prophet, one feels that he was never sufficiently honored "in his own country." Foreign admirers have heaped praises on him and acclaimed him as "the spiritual leader of modern Japan," which he never was. He has been widely respected but has had limited influence within Japan. Why has this been so? It may be partially true to say that the times were not ripe for his message or that the churches were too narrow in their vision for his all-encompassing views. Such conclusions underestimate the spiritual vitality of the Japanese churches, although it is clear that the dominating theological thought of the churches after the 1920's gave little support to Kagawa's social concerns. But whatever the reasons for Kagawa's neglect within Japan, it may be hoped that the dedicated vision of this modern prophet will in time be taken up by others who will be able to build on the firm foundations of Japanese Christianity.

Such a brief historical survey of Japanese Christianity may be noteworthy only for how much has been omitted. A list of other Japanese leaders, missionaries, schools, churches and social work projects that deserve mention would be long indeed. Yet from the lives of these three leaders—an educator, a pastor and a prophet—we may catch some glimpse of both the promises and the problems of modern Japanese Christianity. Since the day a courageous samurai boy sailed out from Edo Harbor, a legacy of rich leadership from the past has developed with which Japanese Christians face the issues of today's world.

2

JAPAN TODAY—WHAT LIES AHEAD?

DAVID L. SWAIN

In the days of despair and bewilderment after the end of World War II, a fledgling playwright named Junji Kinoshita sat in a book-cluttered room in the YMCA dormitory of Tokyo University. A former classmate who had just been demobilized from the Japanese Army in Saigon had dropped in, and during their discussion Kinoshita brought out a copy of a drama he had just written.

Storm-tossed Waves

The drama, entitled *Kazanami* ("Storm-tossed Waves"), is set in the city of Kumamoto. It takes place during the revolutionary decade that followed the Meiji Restoration of 1868, which marked Japan's entry into the modern world. In successive scenes, it reveals various contending schools of thought on how best to steer Japan along her new modern course.

When Japan broke out of 250 years of self-imposed isolation her future was rich with many possibilities, and there were scores of voices proclaiming different directions. What they were talking about amounted to more than empty theories. They were talking about the future of the accustomed patterns of land controls and taxes, about how they would manage their families and raise their children. The issue was the destiny of the entire nation as it was confronted by the overwhelmingly superior might of the Western powers.

A fervent group of Shintōist believers saw this as the time par excellence for Japan to assert her own native religious sentiments. An allied group saw Japan's best advantages as being inherent in a broader context of East Asian values, expressed in Confucianism. A more pragmatically minded group discounted the Confucianists, emphasizing the rapid assimilation of Western technology. Another group seeking relief from landlords and autocratic rule by the military class snatched at the liberal tradition of the West. Finally, a special group urged that no appropriation of the Western values was adequate unless it embraced first the spiritual core of Western culture, the Christian faith.

Meantime the merchant class, less drawn to ideology, proceeded to add capitalistic methods to their already considerable expertise, and set about increasing the national wealth.

The central character of "Storm-tossed Waves," Sayama, is at once attracted to each of these contending groups and repelled by their inability to answer his often-repeated question: What lies beyond all this fervid activity? Each group has a good point to make, and each represents elements that actually went into the making of Japan's modern state. Sayama feels that each dwells too much on immediate plans and leaves unanswered the long-range questions of Japan's identity as a nation and of her ultimate destiny. Confronted by the most sweeping changes Japan had experienced since the introduction of Chinese culture two thousand years before, a sensitive young man inevitably wonders where it will all lead.

The defeat and unconditional surrender of Japan in 1945 posed a similar situation. Playwright Kinoshita was a modern-day Sayama asking his own generation, "What lies ahead?" at a time when the waters were stormier and the clamoring voices more numerous.

For it must be remembered that the defeat was not simply a military setback; it was the collapse of a particular national orthodoxy, which had been built up through the decades. It was the breaking apart of that arrangement of the ingredients of Japanese nationhood chosen by the Japanese themselves. In the wake of this collapse the remnants of all former contending parties rose to press their claims anew.

The crucial message of the *Kazanami* drama should not be missed: *Japan is a highly pluralistic society, and there is no single explanation of how she became what she is. In the storm-tossed present there is yet no single thrust indicating where she is headed.*

Postwar Options for National Direction

MARXISM

Of the voices calling out after the war, none enjoyed greater appeal and authority at first than the rejected contender of the 1920's, Marxism. Of the great numbers of political prisoners held in jails during the 1930's and 1940's, none outnumbered the Marxists. They moved quickly to capitalize on their advantage, gained through suffering and tenacious loyalty to their ideals. Foiled temporarily by certain measures of Occupation policy, including the "Red Purge," they rose to the peak of their power around 1950. Many who had compromised their convictions with demands of the militarist state during the war years were cowed by the Marxists' determined stand. Thousands who had resented the excessive claims of imperial powers remembered well that it was the Marxists who had resisted such claims time and again.

Ironically, one of the postwar events most objectionable to the Marxists contributed to their undoing, namely, the Korean war. The prosperity that ensued from vast expenditures of United States dollars in Japan in procurement programs gave such a boost to the economy and standard of living as to run completely counter to a favorite dogma of Marxism: inevitable poverty under a capitalist system.

Moreover, Japanese sentiment had been repelled by the war experiences. When the Hungarian revolt of 1956 was crushingly suppressed by the Soviets, the image of communism was darkened considerably. In February of that same year, when Nikita Kruschev made his now famous "secret speech" denouncing Stalinist excesses, the decline of Marxist influence in Japan became all the more evident.

The Japanese Marxists themselves had meanwhile engaged in a debate over "autonomy," or whether there could be a unique experience and expression of Marxism in Japan. Counter arguments insisted that Marxism anywhere was

Marxism, and that it meant adherence to orthodox lines, of either Moscow or Peking. The debate still rages and plagues the Japan Communist party, as well as exciting many not formally in the party but attracted to Marxist thinking. In any event, many persons previously drawn by Marxist thought have been lost to the movement in the confusion.

Another major factor in the decline of Marxist influence in Japan in the decade after the war was renewed interaction with the Western world. The Japanese were eager to find out what developments had taken place in all fields, in thought, politics and social life. The existentialist literature of Europe revealed how many of the Europeans had responded to similar wartime experiences. American pragmatism was encountered in the remaking of the Japanese school system under the Occupation.

LIBERAL REFORMS OF THE OCCUPATION

The establishment of democratic institutions under the tutelage of the Occupation was a major factor in releasing the historic energies of liberal concern, long deprived of an opportunity to mold national life. Though these reforms were administered from the top down, they expressed feelings held by many of the Japanese people. The directives of the Occupation authority included the establishment of equality and suffrage for women, land redistribution reform, decentralization of economic power through the dissolution of monopolistic cartels, or *zaibatsu*, and new freedoms for the labor movement. The increased participation in labor unions gave the nation a new channel for stronger mobilization of liberal and progressive ideals.

Perhaps the most significant of the reforms, for the people in general in direct relationship to their government, were three steps which directly reversed the nationalistic orthodoxy of prewar times. These were: the epoch-making renunciation of war as an instrument of national policy in the famous Article 9 of the new constitution; the decentralization of police administration from tight central to dispersed prefectural control; and the overall democratization of public education. The latter meant not only increased opportunity for all and extension of the compulsory school period from six to nine years, but the removal of much of the central government's direct control over teachers, texts and methods.

These three measures expressed a highly significant general characteristic of the postwar era. That trait is a pervasive "peace mood" marking the Japanese as they seek to carve out, through peaceful means, a form of national existence in the international community. It is well known that Japan is as severely restricted in land area that can be cultivated (16 percent of an area slightly smaller than California) as it is overcrowded by its population, the seventh largest and fifth most dense in the world. While contraceptive methods and legalized abortion have acted to reduce overall population increase, the inescapable conditions remain: Japan must supply its people's needs through acquisition of the resources and wealth of the world beyond its own national boundaries.

The new mood of peaceful engagement with other peoples demanded, though, that this acquisition be accomplished in mutually acceptable ways, such as technical exchange and trade, instead of by forceful expansion. A major statesman of a western European republic once greeted former Prime Minister Ikeda of Japan as *sekai no seirusuman*—"Salesman of the world." While this epithet may have carried an embarrassing implication for him and his countrymen, it nonetheless reflected an acknowledgment of the dignity of a people seeking to commend itself to the world in the excellence of its products rather than in the might of its military forces.

CONSERVATIVE REACTIONS

Perhaps it was inevitable that a backswing of the pendulum should have occurred. As the Japanese people groped forward on the unnatural terrain of their democratic and peace-oriented course, feelings of anxiety and frustration grew. Practical difficulties in maintaining internal peace and order motivated the conservative cabinets of the 1950's to seek restoration of some degree of central control in police administration. Sometimes it was almost impossible even to apprehend a criminal. Difficulties in achieving uniform standards in educational administration created pressure for the reinstitution of central controls over education. A highly mobile populace, moving back and forth across Japan's forty-six prefectures, seemed to require greater central administrative controls. Influenced by the demands of the war in Korea, the forming again of large corporations was a dominating feature of the Japanese economy. Finally, the rise of a strong and militant power on the Chinese mainland and the outbreak of the Korean war provided strong arguments for the creation of at least a small self-defense force.

The United States, which had sponsored adoption of the "Peace Constitution," now strongly encouraged the latter move.

These measures, often referred to in the press as the "backward course," were initiated in the late years of the Occupation, which ended in 1952. A crisis was reached under the cabinet of Prime Minister Kishi, when opposition forces rallied to block the renewal of the Japan-United States Mutual Security Pact in 1960. The pact had been agreed upon as a compensation for the end of the Occupation. It granted the United States the right to maintain military bases in Japan, and the United States in turn pledged herself to come to the aid of Japan in case of attack from outside. The opposition Socialist forces saw its continuance as the final breakthrough for the reinstitution of the military arm in the national structure and held widespread demonstrations to block Diet ratification of the pact.

At the peak of this crisis, President Dwight D. Eisenhower was scheduled for a visit to Japan, to commemorate one hundred years of "cultural associations." Determined to deny the prestige of an American president to the Kishi-led maneuvers, the Socialists sponsored nationwide demonstrations, which effectively prevented his visit. The Security Pact was renewed, but Kishi was forced out of office. Encouraged by this partial success, the Socialist forces have set their sights for the renunciation of the Security Pact in 1970, when it becomes legal for either government to alter or void the pact. The Socialists hope to avoid thus any military involvement in the tensions that beset much of Asia today.

The wisdom of this course of action is hotly debated

among many groups today. Awareness of such tensions, however, is a necessary condition for understanding Japanese dissatisfaction with the course of events in Vietnam, the tensions surrounding the normalization of relations with South Korea, and anxiety over the breakdown of Sino-Soviet relations. In short, Japanese opinion ranges over a wide spectrum, from grave doubt to assured confidence, as to whether Japan's new peace posture is sufficient for the years that lie ahead.

SPIRITUAL TRADITIONS OLD AND NEW

The religions. Ideas about the future of Japan have not been limited to attacks by the progressives on the conservatives, calling for reform or revolution. Uncertainty about the future, coupled with a distinct sense of loss of continuity with the past, has found expression in reaffirmations of Japanese spiritual traditions. The more numerous include older religious groups such as Tenrikyō (founded in 1839) and Konkōkyō (1860). Dozens of newer groups have been formed to fill the confused though hardly empty religious forum of the postwar era. One of the best known is the Sōka Gakkai, which has flourished since about 1956, though its roots are prewar.

These faith groups have certainly responded to a deep need among Japan's masses, especially people of farm areas, small shopowners and workers in smaller enterprises. A leading magazine, *The Asahi Journal,* remarked at the beginning of 1965 that, while 1964 showed unparalleled economic growth over previous years, it also showed a record-breaking number of bankruptcies among small firms. The *Journal* indicated that people in businesses vulnerable to bankruptcy had little sense of security in the immediate future; they felt left out of the nation's vigorous recovery from wartime depletion. It was from among these workers that the swollen ranks of the "new religions" were supplied. Undoubtedly the uprooting of family ties in mass migration to the cities helped intensify the sense of no longer belonging. Complicated ideological movements afforded little consolation for less-privileged and less-sophisticated people. The slow results of the new democratic processes, which seem to take years and years to accomplish discernible improvements, left them unsatisfied.

Tenrikyō has established its own university. It and other faith groups are attracting students and also business and government workers. Whether these faith groups will continue to expand or have just about reached a saturation point is not yet clear.

Nihilism. In contrast to the postwar spectrum of varying loyalties and conflicting affirmations, a significant number of sensitive young people have elected to affirm neither past nor future, and yield loyalty to no group or movement in the present. Such negative sophistication is more prevalent in urban areas, among members of the "lonely crowd" who experience little of the social relatedness of former days. Deeply sympathetic with similar expressions of pessimism emanating from disenchanted postwar Europe, these persons express only cynicism with respect to great causes, whether "race," "nation," or even "mankind" or "reason."

Not all of them are irresponsible "beatnik" types by any means. Some are informed, sensitive thinkers who nonetheless suffer vicariously for their own generation and tend to see in nice-sounding slogans and phrases only the false fabrications by which men seek to delude either themselves or their fellows. Beyond well-intentioned and even disciplined labors, there lies for these prophets of gloom only disillusionment and nothingness.

Philosophy. The writers just mentioned fulfill the role, albeit negatively, of the interrogator in *Kazanami*, asking in their own ways, "What lies ahead?" They are not the only ones, however. Professional thinkers deeply involved in the prewar nationalism and just as deeply shaken by its collapse asked the same kinds of questions about national foundations. One of them, philosopher Hajime Tanabe of Kyoto University, published a short paper as an open letter to all would-be reformers, under the title "The Urgent Business of Philosophy." In it he urged on concerned leaders the primary question of the nation's identity and destiny. His plea was that, prior to all efforts for social reconstruction and economic rebuilding, the fundamental question of the basic character and direction of the Japanese people be given some acceptable and workable answer.

Having been one who seriously tried to give definition to the national character in prewar days, and feeling responsible to attempt another answer after the war, Tanabe wrote "Philosophy as Penitence." In this paper, he expressed the desire to implant in the hearts of the Japanese the message that all man's rational efforts, ideas, programs and practices presupposed some commitment to an ultimate concern. Only religion could give a proper idea of what this commitment should be. He called for a new "religious reformation," which would be a blending of the best in democracy, Marxism and religion. While he found his own primary personal guidance in the faith of True Pure Land Buddhism, stemming from the medieval sage Shinran, he proposed inclusion of Kierkegaard's existentialism and the Christian sense of historical relevance and mediating love.

Tanabe's works, like others embodying a sense of urgency about Japan's destiny, were widely read in the immediate postwar years. In the meantime, though, the question of political structure was dealt with in the enactment of the new Constitution on November 3, 1946, and in its promulgation in May of the following year. The daily question which faced everyone was that of food, clothing and shelter. Inevitably the major energies of the Japanese—who are noted for tremendous vitality in times of crisis—were turned to what Tanabe called the "secondary questions" of economic rebuilding and social reconstruction.

The Nation Rebuilds

ECONOMIC RECOVERY

Former United States Ambassador Edwin O. Reischauer has estimated that more than 2 million citizens of the United States have visited or lived in Japan since the end of World War II. Without doubt they have carried back an image of almost unbelievable recovery and advance, beyond even prewar levels of progress.

Economically, the world has witnessed a miracle. With 70 percent of her productive resources destroyed in the war, the Japanese nation showed the world her astonishing capacity for recovery. By 1951 she had regained her prewar level of production; by 1956 the productivity index stood at twice the prewar level; and since that time it has increased by 3.5 times the prewar level. Measured another way, the economic growth rate has averaged about 10 percent a year in recent years. Japan's cement exports lead the world. In the manufacture of radio and television sets Japan is surpassed only by the United States, and her production of crude steel ranks fourth on the economic scoreboard of the world.

In recent years Japan has led the world in shipbuilding, an industry that has been the nation's leading one for many years. She launched 5,363,232 tons gross in 1965, 1,278,042 tons more than in the previous year. Lloyd's Register of Shipping (London) said, "The 1965 figure (12,215,817 tons gross worldwide) is a peacetime record for the second year in succession and this advance . . . rests on the performance of Japan." This performance represented 43.9 percent of the world's output and included two of the 19 ships over 50,000 tons launched in the world. The world's 25 largest ships were oil tankers, the first five of them built in Japan. The largest of all, the *Tokyo Maru*, boasted 96,500 tons gross. Japan's own shipping fleet now ranks fifth in the world.

The importance of shipping is clear from Japan's dependence on her export-import trade to feed her millions. The expansion of her markets across the world has not been uniform, yet they are now fairly equally balanced between the Americas, the Asia-Oceania zone and the Europe-Africa zone. The government's Bureau of Statistics gave these figures for 1964:

Area	Exports (percent)	Imports (percent)
Americas	34.07	24.89
Asia-Oceania	30.81	25.04
Europe-Africa	14.50	16.88

Trade relations with the Soviet Union have been restored; and they have been renewed with the People's Republic of China, though many diplomatic delicacies remain to endanger the latter channel. Even so, export-import trade with China is reported to have doubled from 1964 to 1965. The volume of this trade is still infinitesimal compared to Japan's trade with the United States and Canada, which remains the primary source of current prosperity in Japan. Her trade with Canada in 1964 amounted to $545,000,000, Japan's largest volume of trade with any single nation except the United States. In the same year, trade with the U.S. amounted to $4,178,000,000.

Immediately after the war Japan's foreign trade depended almost entirely on the United States. Exports to the U.S. in 1946 ran to 65 percent and imports from the U.S. totaled 86 percent. These figures have leveled off to 28 percent for exports and 29 percent for imports in 1964.

The two million Americans who have been in Japan since the war include many who understand the importance of the United States market to the Japanese economy. The fact is that Japan is the United States' number two customer, second only to Canada. If trade relations alone guaranteed international security, Japan-United States relations might remain fairly secure for some time to come. The one lesson that should be abundantly clear by now, though, is that history is always complex. No single thread dominates its intricate patterns. The economic fiber is only part of the larger fabric.

Japan's economy, in spite of its remarkable record, is still quite vulnerable. The country depends on international trade for most of the raw materials essential to her manufacturing industries. The drive toward increased productivity has absorbed most of Japan's resources and talent; only a small percentage has been spared for research and capital accumulation. Japan must still look to the West for leadership in technological advances, and most of her industries operate within the limits of extensive capital loan arrangements.

According to the Bank of Tokyo *Weekly Review*, May 9, 1966, during 1965 capital loans secured from foreign financial institutions amounted to $379,551,000, a sharp drop from the $650,760,000 that were secured during 1964. The decline in 1965 reflected the temporary recession in the Japanese economy. Foreign investments in Japan approved during 1965 dropped to a total of $528,506,000, compared with a total of $912,785,000 in 1964.

Even if these handicaps are overcome—and the evidence indicates that they will be—the question still comes from within Japan's core of thinkers and writers: Does a full stomach make a whole man? It is an age-old question known around the world, as to whether it is worth living in order to work, or working in order to live, and so on in a meaningless circle. The size of the middle class, in 1964 estimated to be 69 percent of Japan's population, increases yearly as the extremes between wealth and poverty are reduced; yet it is this class of people especially who buy the current crop of books that seek a definite answer to the query, "What lies ahead?"

While production needs absorbed the attention and energies of the nation after the war, the economy gradually provided ample surplus for long-deprived consumers. Net national income in 1946 dropped to 51 percent of the prewar standard, but it recovered quickly, registering 15 percent above the prewar standard by 1951 and 201 percent by 1963. Of course, price rises have been astronomical too, compared to the prewar consumer price index. Even so, although the ratio of expenditures for food among urban dwellers right after the war was 60 percent of total income, by 1964 it was 38 percent, leaving a greater proportion of income for housing and clothing, as well as for educational, cultural and other pursuits. The general employment index jumped 34 percent during the 1960-1964 period alone, even though the labor force increased by about 5 million between 1955 and 1963. The average work week of about 46 hours ranks with France, just under the United Kingdom and just above West Germany. Urban households, constituting 64 percent of the nation by 1960, are able to save about 20 percent of their income.

It is one of the ironies of human life that stable economic conditions permitting relative faith in the *near* future (for which people will put aside 20 percent of their earnings) tend to obscure the importance of longer-range questions of basic identity and ultimate destiny. Japan shares the problem of the spiritually numbing effects of affluence with many of the other advanced nations.

POLITICAL LIFE

The Liberal-Democratic party. Politically it is not so much the scarcity of questions as the bumper crop of answers that is striking. To be sure, with the exception of a single Socialist government after the war (1947-1948), the conservatives have maintained their political domination and have given the country a continuity of policy and power. Yet their designation, Liberal-Democrat, is often written with a hyphen; and it covers a plurality of factions. Only the highly informed observer can follow the intricate gradings of factionalism on which their power rests. From time to time dissension in the ranks erupts to threaten their hold over the political fortunes of the nation.

The opposition. The opposition parties deride the Liberal-Democrats sorely for opportunism about immediate goals and for the retention of power. These parties propose varying degrees of radical change. Yet the Socialists are not without dissension and factions themselves. Their overall influence was somewhat dissipated by a break in 1959 which resulted in the formation of a splinter group, the Democratic Socialist party. The latter espouses a moderate middle-of-the-road stance, while the larger Socialist party ranges widely from near center to far left. The extreme left is nervously guarded by the numerically small Japan Communist party, which follows a pattern similar to that of the Socialists by engaging in intense controversy over "purist" positions allied to Peking or "revisionist" factions inclined toward Moscow. The leadership position won in the 1960 student demonstrations by Marxist-oriented student groups was lost within half a year because of arguments about the exercise of that leadership. One faction in the *Zengakuren*, the National Students' Self-Government Association, even stoned the Japan Communist party headquarters to punish that party for deviation from purist lines.

Sensitivity to the lack of a working consensus in the political arena has sharpened among various segments of society. It is hardly surprising that one of the more militant religious groups, the Sōka Gakkai, should seek to provide some resolution to the confused, and sometimes corrupt, political scene. Extending its hand formally into national political life in 1962, its candidates for the Upper House of the Diet won 4,120,000 votes, or 11.2 percent of the total vote. The 20 Diet members of its political organization, the *Kōmei-tō,* rank third in the Upper House, coming after the Liberal-Democrat membership of 140 and the Socialist membership of 73. Aiming also for the more important Lower House and avowedly determined to gain a majority by 1980, its brand of political salvation is proffered to the nation in preference to the introduction of outside elements. It reaffirms its own version of the Buddhist tradition derived from the teachings of the twelfth century leader Nichiren.

To what extent this group will appeal to more of the Japanese population than the 4.3 million families already claimed remains to be seen. Any guesses must be tempered by remembering that other strong religious groups claim validity for their own versions of national succor, and that unnumbered millions are indifferent to religion of any sort. Many reject religious claims on social and political life. If politics is "the art of the possible," the claims of the fanatically sure may have rough sledding ahead; though on the other hand, only two decades separate this generation from one singularly given to absolutism. For the present, however, the "urgent business" proposed by Tanabe—a search for the nation's basic identity and ultimate destiny—remains strangely absent from everyday political life.

SOCIAL AND CULTURAL LIFE

The plurality that marks political groupings is but a pale reflection of the fantastic diversity in social and cultural life. Most Western visitors have long since graduated from the simple image of Japan as characterized exclusively by cherry trees, geisha girls and Mount Fuji. They know of Japan's new super-express that travels the 345-mile distance from Tokyo to Osaka in 3 hours and 10 minutes. The prestige of the prize-winning Honda motorcycles of international fame now equals the reputation long enjoyed by excellent Japanese cameras. Many remember that in the 1964 Olympic Games in Tokyo Japan won more medals than any other country, except for the perennially dominant U.S.A. and U.S.S.R. The Olympic Games afforded many people an opportunity, directly or through news media, for visual appreciation of truly impressive architectural achievements in Japan, marvelously blending East and West. If the harrowing traffic excited many an unaccustomed adrenal gland, it also revealed Japan as a top producer of automotive vehicles, ranking second to the United States in production of commercial vehicles. Its established Toyota Corporation rose to membership, even though bottom place, in the world's top ten producers in 1965.

These better-known symbols of Japan's postwar prosperity are only the more obvious items of a general social process that has brought improved welfare to the Japanese people. It is these people, however, who must be given credit for the vitality, intelligence and assiduity that produced it. For instance, the fear of unattended death or deterioration of health has been largely eliminated, as approximately 98 percent of the total population are recipients of benefits under the health insurance system. Nor is this a desk plan without substance. The ratio of 8 hospital beds per 1,000 persons is just below the United States ratio of 9 (6.8 in Canada, 11 in the United Kingdom, 15 in France), and the ratio of 903 persons per doctor is not far above that of 645 for the United States and 865 for Canada.

Urbanization. World War II left a severe housing shortage, and in many areas housing has not kept pace with the growing population. As late as 1963 surveys showed that more than 2 million households suffered from inadequate housing. Yet in 1964 alone more than 751,000 dwellings were constructed, and today's ratio of residents per dwelling is 5, as compared to 3 in the United States, France and Sweden.

The most significant development with respect to housing is the mushrooming of *danchi*, multilevel apartment-house "new towns" now common in the suburbs of all the larger cities. In some cases whole towns have been created to house as many as 150,000 residents. All the concomitants of urbanization found elsewhere affect the Japanese population. The problems of food supply, educational facilities and transportation lines tax public administrators as sorely in Japan's burgeoning metropolitan areas as they do in those of the

United States and Europe. The sameness, the lost sense of identity resulting from cut family ties, the problems of juvenile delinquency prompt serious discussions in Japan, too.

For historical perspective, though, it should be pointed out that city life is not a product of the modern age in Japan. The country's ancient capital of Nara (seventh to ninth centuries) is said to have had some 200,000 people. The castle towns of the Middle Ages drew together large populations. The population of the premodern capital Edo (present-day Tokyo) is estimated to have surpassed one million residents, making it probably the world's largest city in the nineteenth century, with runners-up London, Paris, Vienna, Moscow and Berlin ranging from 864,000 to 170,000.

Japanese history has in many respects been dominated by politics. It was the political importance of Nara and Edo, not their marketplaces, that drew together large concentrations of people. Edo's population swelled because of a government requirement that all provincial rulers and their families spend half of each year in the capital, with their many attendants. These large political centers were highly integrating forces in urban and national life. The cities were structured along hierarchical lines, determining where people should live and how large or small their dwellings should be. Each administrative, religious and military organization had its assigned place. Success in modern industrialization was made possible partly by the existence of large, well-functioning cities.

Today the feudal patterns of strict assignment of people to places has diminished greatly. Job placement and advancement according to social status and family connection is giving way to selection and promotion according to personal abilities. This is required if Japan is to keep abreast of world competition based on technological skills and managerial competence. The best men must be found and used, no matter what their pedigree. Through such principles, the independence of the individual has been strengthened, as have the prospects of democratic structures.

If this picture of Japan today appears too heavily oriented toward city life, it is because urban change is the dominant feature in an overall transformation of the total society. Farm life down to the smallest hamlet has been affected. The manpower shortage in industry has worked its way into the remotest village, drawing rural youth away from home. Because small farmers are pressed for lack of hands, light machinery, fertilizers and insecticides have come into widespread use, and have proven more economical and productive. Traditional patterns have given way to emphasis on commercial gain. If prices for agricultural products drop off, livestock and poultry are introduced.

The inexorable pull of the cities draws men into part-time jobs, leaving wives to work the fields with the help of grandparents or children. On the average nearly half of rural income comes from nonagricultural work. Most important, the values of rural youth are urban-oriented, looking toward educational success and city jobs, and farm girls rarely want to be farmers' wives. The TV "window" has done much to let the young person on the farm know that the rest of Japan is not like his village. Television reaches nearly 70 percent of the rural homes.

The road of modern transformation has not been smooth throughout society. Resistance to change is deeply rooted in government, business, social and especially rural life. Modernization was carried out from the top down in Japan, and the overriding considerations were mainly political, not matters of a common faith expressing itself.

Changes in family life. Nowhere is change a more painful fact than in family life. Family patterns in former times were father-centered; whether father knew best or not, he was always judged to be right. His position of authority in the family was a microcosm of the larger social order, whether in a business firm where the boss was autocratic or in the state which was viewed as one large family under the Emperor. Today the father's job still demands his loyalty, leaving him little time to explore new patterns commensurate with the new ideas flowing in and exciting interest. Education and recreation for the children are "farmed out" to professional agencies. Little time or place remains to the family to evolve as a renewed unit of democratic society.

One interest does bind the parents to their children— the necessity for education. It is common to recognize that good jobs follow graduation from the "best" schools. The parental flurry to assure entrance into certain kindergartens because they have connections with prestigious schools is astounding.

Education. Enthusiasm for education in Japan is hardly limited to purely utilitarian ends, nor is it a recent element of the nation's culture. Temple schools were the primary agencies of training centuries ago. In the immediately premodern Edo period, Confucianism was made the official ideology of the government. Its great legacy was a respect for learning and a disciplined attitude toward acquiring knowledge. Few factors have been as important as these in enabling the Japanese to appropriate Western knowledge and skills rapidly and effectively in the years since the Meiji Restoration in 1868.

The Meiji leaders made compulsory schooling a part of their program of national transformation. Consequently, the percentage of school-age children enrolled jumped from 28 percent in 1873 to 81 percent by 1900, and climbed to more than 99 percent by 1920, where it has remained since. While higher education was intentionally reserved for an elite class, increasing from 1.23 percent of the total youth population in 1920 to only 3.01 percent in 1940, its quality was excellent. Students and professors alike today look back with nostalgia and envy on the old universities.

Just the same, the remarkable changes achieved after the war should not be underestimated—indeed, they were revolutionary! With the further emancipation of women under the Occupation, for instance, the enrollment of girls in upper secondary schools (high schools), beyond the compulsory level, doubled in the decade from 1950 to 1960. The proportion of the total youth population reaching higher educational institutions jumped to 10.67 percent by 1962. Not only does a much larger proportion of the population receive more education than ever before, but it does so at a time when the population scale bulges at the 10-20 years age level. Illiteracy, an effective yardstick of educational results, has virtually been eliminated. More important, perhaps, for a state depending on complex industrial, trade and diplomatic arrangements extending around the world, some 70 percent advance beyond the compulsory junior high level to high school, and about 30 percent of the high school graduates continue on to colleges and universities.

Mass communications. The remarkable thing about the Japanese is not that everyone *can* read but that most *do!* Japan's *Asahi Shimbun* has the largest circulation of any single newspaper in the world, and the combined newspaper circulation of 43,802,000 is exceeded only by the more populous United States. This figure, however, represents only the broad base of the nation's reading habits. Weeklies and journals, highbrow and low, numbered 14,049 in 1960, though they dropped to 7,233 in 1962. According to available statistics, the number of books published in Japan is surpassed only by that of the U.S.S.R., the United Kingdom, the United States and West Germany.

Quantitative distinctions are not so impressive at the level of serious reading as are the marks of quality. Journals of 200 to 400 pages monthly reveal the groping for ideas to stir up or solve the complicated questions of a complex society and a problem-ridden world. In addition to Japan's own literature, novelists of every major nation are widely translated and read—Maugham, Faulkner, Greene, Proust, Sartre and so on. Debates over Hegel, Marx, Mao Tse-tung or Kierkegaard are commonplace among university students, and even among the alumni now graduated and occupying posts in business and government.

Completing the mass media picture, radio stations have multiplied to 436, far more than the 3 stations in 1925 when broadcasting was first begun in Japan. Television coverage has been extended to 90 percent of the population (98 percent in the cities), with an average of one set per 1.4 households. Television has made serious inroads into motion picture attendance, which dropped from a yearly per capita rate of 12 in 1958 to only 4 in 1964. Still, with full-length film production running well over 600 in 1963 (nearly three times the nearest competitor, Hong Kong), Japan is still the top film-producing country of the world. And 267 feature films were imported in this same year! Qualitatively, the best Japanese films have gained world renown.

Elizabeth Vining, an American tutor to Japan's Crown Prince some years ago, wrote a book of her experiences, *Windows for the Crown Prince*. The vast facilities of Japan's mass media provide innumerable windows for his peers. They both create and fulfill demands arising from an intense world consciousness. This awareness of Japan's place in, yet apart from, the rest of the world feeds on the Japanese sense of a unique tradition, the implications of the "peace mood," and the pragmatic necessity to sustain life for more than 98 million people through world trade. Translations of the world's literature abound; the flow of ideas into Japan is possibly unparalleled elsewhere in the world. Culturally located between East and West, North and South, sharing problems and possibilities with each global region, Japan is a unique intellectual receptacle.

What Lies Ahead?

Much as the United States was a "melting pot" of the peoples of the world as they flowed a century or more ago into its cities and open spaces seeking new life, so *Japan in*

the twentieth century has become a "melting pot of ideas"
of the world.

A particularly notable aspect of this perspective on Japanese life is the fact that new layers of cultural inflow rarely displace older layers. Shintō, the native religious sentiment stretching back into the earliest days of Japanese history, still lives. The coming of Buddhism in the seventh century in full force, and its diffusion among the masses in the twelfth century, did not smother Shintō. Though the two religions differ immensely, they were combined eventually in a theory of "double aspect." Confucianism was introduced officially in antiquity along with Buddhism but became rooted and influential only in the 300 years preceding the nation's entrance into modern statehood in 1868. Emphasizing social responsibilities and ethical virtues, it shared the Japanese mind and soul with Shintō and Buddhism. Its influence on Japanese thinking even today is indisputable.

The influx of Western science, religion and systems of thought, from Marxism to various forms of humanism, has not displaced the older traditions. Rather, it has added new layers to the complex and fluid body of Japanese thought and religion. We might fear that Christianity would become entangled in the same configuration. On the other hand, without some kind of engagement with these many layers of Japanese cultural life, Christianity may never penetrate beyond a shallow level.

Intensely concerned to know about the world of ideas and movements, Japan as a nation has manifested little readiness to make deep-reaching commitments to any of them. Indeed, the postwar era has thus far been marked by a persistent isolation from world involvement, except in trade relations.

A similar situation exists internally. Individual and group adherence to a set of ideas or a system of beliefs can be tenacious indeed; yet such groups, more often than not, exist in a kind of mutual insularity with regard to each other. Political scientist Masao Maruyama, a leading critic of Japanese cultural life, has likened this propensity to the *tako tsubo*, a narrow-necked flask used in trapping the octopus. Once in, he rarely gets out; nor does he from then on converse with his fellows. Christians are often sensitive about their minority status; yet they are not alone. There are literally thousands of small religious, intellectual and cultural groups that have intense, even tense, relations with members inside the group. But they are virtually isolated from mass involvement or fruitful dialogue with other groups. These groups include everything from poetry recital groups to exotic faith groups and tennis clubs. The expansion of any one group or the proliferation of new groups rarely constitutes a threat of very serious proportions to any of the others.

Lack of mutual encounter is often mistaken by outsiders for general tolerance, which in part it may well be. Intramural conflict, however, is hardly unknown. The number of Buddhist groups adhering to the Lotus Sutra tradition alone, for example, number half a hundred. Divisions within the Christian churches stem partly from the Western background of denominationalism, but not from this alone. They could be said to be, rather, a kind of "indigenization" of the church according to Japanese patterns of small group insularity. Against this backdrop, the formation and persistence of a United Church of Christ in Japan is an ecumenical achievement of the first order, which has few counterparts around the world.

The lack of communication, not to mention integration, among religious groups has not been by any means ignored by the Japanese leaders. Attempts at synthesis have been made, but more often than not these efforts have resulted merely in syncretism. One new religious group, *Seichō-no-Ie*, includes elements of Jewish, Christian, Islamic, Buddhist and Shintō symbolism in its own symbol. One might recall here Tanabe's call for a new "religious reformation," aimed essentially at synthesis.

Despite this plurality and variety of thought, religious and political activities all function within a common atmosphere. Each group breathes the same air as all the others. Whether radical or conservative, pragmatist or spiritualist tendencies predominate, the Japanese mind is marked by an essential sensitivity, which is responsive to delicate aesthetic distinctions, on the one hand, and to the broad range of human problems on the other.

There is a general commitment to "welfare." The long-incumbent conservatives have included in their platform such progressive welfare measures as social security, public health insurance and public housing programs. The peace mood is another element in the common atmosphere. The Japanese shared in an exhausting and devastating war, from which they recoiled as a people. Except for the Marxists, all major cultural and religious associations supported the nationalistic war program—though there were stellar instances of opposition by individual Christians and others. Today the same major groups all strongly favor peace—though there are some disturbing exceptions among rabid rightists. Far from merely exposing the Japanese as a "nation of sheep," this inclination is evidence of a common revulsion from the mutually experienced horrors and sufferings of war. The peace mood may precipitate a common commitment to search for a valid national identity. The wide and avid reading, the widespread desire to travel abroad, the warm welcome offered visitors all reveal a stirring, an openness to new possibilities, coupled with a hope of preserving cherished cultural traditions.

A group of prominent scholars, turning careful attention to this fervid activity of the mind and spirit behind the more readily recognized accomplishments in sports, industry and world trade, characterized the postwar inner world of the Japanese as a time of "groping and confusion." The melting pot still boils; the nature of the final brew is not yet clear. What sort of synthesis or consensus, if any, will issue from the complexity and diversity of possible answers is undecided, but whatever decisions are made will be crucial in the life of the nation. So far, the burden is one of an inability to make a satisfactory peace with the past or to grasp the future with conviction.

Barring some international catastrophe that would damage the economy seriously, the standard of living of the Japanese people is likely to improve. With this, the lingering question intensifies: What is one living for? We began with the *Kazanami* drama that focused on the storm-tossed times of the postwar era. We see a Japan today that rides the crests of massive waves filled with possibilities for progress, yet churned by undercurrents of implicit danger. Can it be that the disturbing energies as well as the enabling forces are indeed of God's making? Perhaps there is an answer to "What lies ahead?" that is discernible to the eyes of faith.

3

THE CHRISTIAN MOVEMENT
IN JAPAN TODAY

YOICHIRO SAEKI

No Japanese Christian today can escape from the reality that he is a member of a tiny minority in the nation. The total number of Christian people in Japan, including Protestant, Roman Catholic and Orthodox believers, is only some 800,000 out of a total population of nearly 100,000,000. Protestant believers number 443,709 (or approximately one percent of the nation's population), Roman Catholic believers 314,451 and Eastern Orthodox believers 15,000. Of the total number of Protestant believers, the membership of the United Church of Christ in Japan, including communicant and inactive members, comprises 193,435. Protestant Christianity has 5,472 organized churches and preaching centers, the Roman Catholic Church 760 and the Orthodox Church 105. The ordained and licensed ministers of Protestant Christianity number 5,348. Priests of the Roman Catholic Church, including foreign priests, total 1,772. There are 65 Eastern Orthodox priests.[1]

Christianity and the Japanese Scene

In considering the difficulties of evangelism, the basic problems are those common to the church throughout the world. They are distinct enough, however, in the setting of Japan, that we can speak in a sense of "Japanese problems." There is a striking similarity in the issues faced by the different churches—Protestant, Roman Catholic and Orthodox alike—in Japan. Lutherans in Japan, for example, have more in common with Episcopalians in Japan than with Lutherans in other lands. The differences in ecclesiastical traditions that were brought in from the West are part of the picture. A few issues, however, which are particularly pertinent to the Christian movement in Japan, may be described.

ADULT BAPTISM

Most Protestant churches in Japan follow the practice of adult baptism, while the major part of Western Christianity, in contrast, practices infant baptism. Being baptized at birth, most people in Western countries become automatically Christian. For hundreds of years this situation has been taken for granted, and it is the basis of the *Corpus Christianum*.

In principle, adult baptism requires a spontaneous and responsible decision on the part of the candidate. In the early days of the Christian movement in Japan, and in some cases even now, becoming a Christian meant a total break with the rest of the family. One sees here the same reality that Jesus described to his disciples—that he came to set a man against his father, and a daughter against her mother and a daughter-in-law against her mother-in-law, and that a man's foes will be the members of his own household. Adult baptism means a man's complete separation from his old way of life, which was centered around self-interest, and his living with Christ the Lord within the communion of the church, the Body of Christ.

In the history of Protestant Christianity in Japan, there is no instance of a mass conversion such as those that occurred in Europe when entire populations, following the example of their king or leader, were baptized. The same type of mass conversion has occasionally happened in modern times. In Japan, however, the gospel has customarily been heard and studied by individuals for a year on the average, before they have made a clear decision to receive baptism. Even more thorough prebaptismal training is emphasized today, to prepare people to live as Christians in a non-Christian world.

Western Christendom, along with Japanese Buddhism and Shintō, gives much food for thought to Japanese Christians concerning what it means to be a majority religion. Historically, it is an accepted view that Buddhism became a majority religion only after it had compromised with the power and wealth of society. In the West, infant baptism has obscured the line of distinction between the church and the world. Society itself is sometimes called a Christian society, which it can never be. The basic question is: How many Christians are necessary for the salvation of the nation? Even if all of Japan's people should become Christians, there is no guarantee that the nation would be saved if they were self-centered, as many present-day Christians are. Abraham asked the Lord how many righteous men were necessary for the salvation of Sodom and Gomorrah, and the answer was narrowed down to ten. (See Genesis 18.) The really important issue is whether the existing minority is leaven for the lump and salt for the earth, or whether it is not.

THE RISE OF AUTHENTIC SECULARISM

A second basic problem for Christianity in Japan is the rise of authentic paganism, or secularism. Since the end of World War II, Japanese religions have been suffering from a great tide of secularization. For example, in Nagoya, the third largest city in Japan, Buddhist cemetery lots had to be moved from the temples to the suburbs as a result of city planning. Consequently, the laity found it unnecessary to visit their temples, for they could go directly to the cemetery and hold memorial services without the assistance of priests. Thus, the priests are experiencing a severe loss of lay support and are having to depend on sales of land holdings for their living, without being able to revitalize their religious activities.

Sōka Gakkai, a militant Buddhist sect (described in the preceding chapter), is not a religious movement in the usual sense, but rather a political movement for that segment of people which does not have representation in the existing political parties. In this sense it is a pseudo-religion. Risshō Kōseikai, another new Buddhist movement, is also a lay association, which provides fellowship and counseling in small groups. In other words, traditional Buddhism is gradually losing its religious influence, and new and resurgent

Buddhism derives its strength from either political activities or fellowship groups.

Statistics on Japan's religions are notably unreliable. A recent religious census showed that there are 140,000,000 believers of all religions in Japan, whereas the total population is only 97,350,000! A more realistic estimate is that there are approximately 20,000,000 practicing believers in various religions. Thus, four-fifths of the total population is nonreligious. More and more it is recognized that there are sincere, authentic and responsible people among the nonreligious. Modern secular culture is no lower than so-called Christian culture, and thus the Christian mission today in Japan is not a crusade of the cultured aimed at the less cultured.

In Japan today, this nonreligious secularism is making a great contribution to the development and maturity of the nation. For centuries, people in Japan were in bondage to religious traditions and observances that endowed natural objects, persons, social structures and other phenomena with a veil of holiness. Secularization stripped away this veil and set people free from the bondage of religions. Secularization requires people to live as men and to face human problems with human integrity, not with the false assumption that hidden mysterious religious powers have control over human affairs.

The first-rate schools and hospitals are secular institutions. Christian schools are sometimes second rate, though schools for women rank higher than schools for men. Works of St. Augustine and Sören Kierkegaard are being translated by non-Christians; and church music by Bach and Handel is played by secular musicians with outstanding professional competence.

The Christian church must ask a basic and realistic question: Why is Christian faith necessary in an authentic secular society? What is the heart of the Christian message, which must be proclaimed to a sophisticated, cultured non-religious people who are doing very well in human life and society?

MARXISM AND EXISTENTIALISM

The third problem Christians in Japan are facing today is that most of the Japanese intelligentsia read Karl Marx and Jean Paul Sartre before they read the Bible. The Bible and portions from the Bible have been the principal best-sellers for years, selling about four million copies a year. Karl Marx and Marxism, or Jean Paul Sartre and atheistic existentialism, may be called devilish children of Western Christianity. Seen as antitheses and criticisms of Christianity, they are meaningful in Western culture. Secular thinkers in Japan, however, read them before they read the Bible and before they hear the church's proclamation of the gospel.

They also read the history of Western civilization, especially of so-called Christian civilization, which is marked by war, crusades, colonization and exploitation. The basic question in this case is whether Christianity brings peace and happiness to life and solutions to the problems of Japan.

Japan is facing the front-line problems of Christianity in the world today. The church has to answer the questions raised by a secular society in the course of its evangelistic efforts. If it fails to answer them and becomes just one more religion among others, seeking primarily an increase of members, Christianity in Japan will have lost its reason for existence.

Contemporary Challenges Before Japanese Churches

Keeping the above context in mind, let us turn to the work of the Christian churches in Japan today. Evangelism has been most difficult in rural areas, because in rural areas there have been thick walls of feudalistic social and mental structures based upon the family system. In the past, all behavior was watched by the community, and therefore people in rural Japan were not free from community ties and obligations. Thus, it was extremely difficult for ordinary rural people to go to Christian meetings. It took years for a man to become a Christian, for he faced many kinds of opposition on all sides. It was by no means easy for an evangelist to secure a foothold in a rural community without devoting decades to living as a member of the community.

In cities, however, people have been more free from traditional ties and community interference, and have consequently found it easier to change their way of life. Thus the atmosphere of the city is an easier one for Christian evangelism. Most city churches in Japan have been formed not by a geographical division of the total responsibility of the mission of the church, but by people who have had personal connections with a pastor or who have been attracted by the sermons of a particular preacher. Therefore the character of a congregation has been more that of a relationship of disciples to their teacher, rather than of parishioners to their pastor.

POPULATION MOBILITY

The church has suffered from population mobility in rural areas. In communities where pastors stayed in one place for decades and put their whole lives into evangelizing the community, sometimes with the assistance of missionaries, the influence of the church has been felt. But where pastors have changed often, Christianity has remained an outside influence. Thus, the church has by and large been unable to reach the stable people of rural communities. It has tended to reach only the mobile wage earners and the youth who move to the cities after completing their high school education.

The same sort of difficulty has prevailed among city churches. Downtown and inner city churches are suffering from the fact that their members move out to suburban residential areas. There has been an extensive population expansion in the suburban areas of large cities, with so-called "new towns" and high-rise apartment houses. Naturally, there has appeared the need for the placement of new churches. Generally, when a new church is started in Japan it begins around the nucleus of a few persons who are already Christians. It has been suggested in recent years that the members of downtown and inner city churches who do not live in the vicinity of their own church should transfer their membership to the suburban churches in the neighborhoods where they live. Such a suggestion may sound strange to Christians in the West, but it reveals important issues before Christianity in the present-day Japanese world.

Proponents of the idea that a Christian should belong to

the local congregation in his residential community maintain that downtown and inner city churches which are unwilling to encourage their members to transfer their membership are too preoccupied with self-preservation. Opponents of this idea maintain that strategically the existence and prosperity of any downtown church is an important symbol of the work of the church in the whole country. An active membership that supports the work of downtown churches is therefore necessary in order to reach multitudes of people who would not otherwise come in contact with the church. Furthermore, many inner city areas have deteriorated for residential purposes and have lost stable people of middle-class background. They serve mainly as ports of entry for many single young people who come from the country to secure jobs in the cities. Therefore, these areas are usually unstable and face problems such as low incomes, inadequate and substandard housing, juvenile delinquency, slum dwellings, poor social welfare benefits and inferior schools. If the churches in inner city areas must be supported only by those members who live there, they can hardly perform active service for the needs of the community, nor can they carry on effective evangelism. In Tokyo there are 23 wards. Meguro and Shinagawa are typical inner city wards, whereas Setagaya and Suginami are suburban wards. The number of inhabitants per pastor (counting all Christian groups) in each of these wards is: Meguro, 15,497; Shinagawa, 20,530; Setagaya, 7,778; and Suginami 7,915. This situation means that the churches in the inner city are expected to carry out heavier responsibilities, since there are more churches and ministers in the suburbs.

SELF-CENTERED FAITH

One of the crucial challenges for Japanese Christianity is that faith has become very much a matter for private life, or for family life at the most. It seldom extends to the sphere of public life in society. This tendency has two causes: one is the disintegration of the *Corpus Christianum*, and the other is a too-close relationship between a person's residence and his church membership. In a country like Japan, in which there has never really been a *Corpus Christianum*, it has not been easy for Christianity to exercise influence on society at large. Thus, when a Christian goes to church in his own neighborhood, church life is in danger of becoming primarily a part of his private life, especially in the urban situation.

The separation of residence and working place is one of the primary characteristics of urbanization, and it has contributed to the disintegration of the old feudalistic social structure and the religions that supported it. Without the separation of residence and working place, people could not have become emancipated from the country's traditionally tight social structure. In the old feudalistic society, every communal event was the private affair of those in power, even in political matters. In cities, where the separation is nearly complete, every event has more of a public character than in a rural community.

The same situation holds true in church life. Churches where most members live and work in the same place, for example, in rural, mining, small industry and suburban areas, have a character of privateness. They offer an atmosphere of familiarity, at-homeness and stability, yet lack public concern.

In the history of Christianity in Japan, Christian churches and gifted laymen have exercised significant influence on public opinion by leading in such areas as social welfare, education, prohibition of prostitution, emphasis on monogamy and creation of literature and music. Most of the influence, however, has come from certain prophetic preachers around whom strong churches were formed, regardless of the commuting distance of the members. On the other hand, the life of the common people in Japan was influenced not by these outstanding preachers but by small, local churches whose main concerns were the sphere of private lives, salvation of individual souls, peace of mind and the like. Here lies the dilemma of the church in Japan, and the problems before the church.

The major Protestant churches have recognized this challenge, and in recent years they have adapted their evangelistic policies to deal with it. There are two main issues in evangelistic policy. One is that of enabling a local church to step out of its own private self-interest and become concerned about the public aspects of the life of society, that is, with the course of national and world history. The other is that of enabling a church which has such an interest in public affairs to spread its influence and carry out evangelism in its local community among residents and workers of all ages and social levels. The United Church of Christ in Japan has expressed this clearly in its Ten Year Evangelism Plan, and other major denominations are aiming at the same goal. Smaller groups are somewhat different in their concern, as we can see in the Second Five Year Advance Movement of the Japan Baptist Convention, which is affiliated with the Southern Baptist Convention in the United States of America. For small Christian groups and denominations with a limited distribution of churches and preaching points throughout the country, it is natural to be concerned mainly with church extension and the building up of local congregations.

Specific Churches and Groups

THE UNITED CHURCH OF CHRIST IN JAPAN (KYŌDAN)

The United Church of Christ in Japan, usually called the Kyōdan, was formed in 1941. In its formation there was pressure from society and from government. We should not forget, however, that Protestant Christianity in Japan began in a spirit of nondenominational unity. Even after the formation of denominations, efforts toward unity continued through the Federation of Christian Churches and later through the National Christian Council. This was particularly true after 1928, when the National Council set up a commission for the study and promotion of church union. In 1929 a tentative plan of union was offered by this commission, and discussion began. Though the 15th General Assembly of the Council in 1937 adopted the revised findings of the study commission, before churches were ready to move toward self-defined unity the government's Religious Bodies Law was enacted. The United Church emerged in some measure in response to this act.

Much of what is usually accomplished beforehand had to take place after the union, and in a real sense after the war. It took almost twenty-five years for people from different backgrounds to come to know and understand each other. Only then was the stage reached when people could act by consensus decision. For a long time committee meetings and assemblies could not produce effective plans or achieve results in the field of evangelism. The United Church, for example, deeply regrets that it was not prepared for the great opportunity immediately following World War II, when many people came to the churches looking for a new direction in life. Statistics of church growth show a peak in the year 1951, soon after the Korean war broke out.

The major evangelistic efforts during the period 1950 to 1960 consisted of mass meetings led by evangelists from the West. Many people heard these addresses, but they went away without understanding much of what had been said. Another effort was in pioneer evangelism, with 170 new churches and preaching points established in ten years, in addition to the 1,400 churches then existing. Most of the newly established churches are very small, however, and still need subsidy from outside sources. Congregations of the United Church now total 1,608. In terms of self-support the congregations of the United Church are in a proportion similar to that of the Japanese festival for children seven, five and three years of age ("Shichi-go-San")—seven churches that need subsidy, five barely self-supporting and three self-supporting and capable of assisting others.

In 1961, a heated argument broke out within Protestant circles concerning the Tokyo Christian Crusade of the World Vision movement, headed by Dr. Bob Pierce. At the time there was criticism of church leaders who were said to have neglected responsible, long-term planning for evangelism in favor of general meetings for mass evangelism planned and sponsored by foreigners. The controversy sounded nationalistic on the surface, but in reality it was a demand for responsible planning. It was a turning point for the churches in Japan, and it encouraged the United Church to establish a basic policy for the mission of the church, along with a Ten-year Plan of Evangelism.

The Ten-year Plan of Evangelism aims at the renewal of the United Church, first by the strengthening of lay training, second by the gradual retraining of pastors and third by strengthening the staff at church headquarters for the planning and execution of church policies. The Ten-year Plan has also taken steps for the strengthening of small churches, according to the concrete needs of each situation rather than a general plan. The heart of the plan is the "Evangelistic Area" emphasis. In the West, the idea of either a geographical or a sociological parish is well defined. In Japan, however, it has been little recognized that a local church should take responsibility for a certain geographical area around it. Even in America, a local church serves a certain sociological group of people in an area. In the pluralistic society of urban Japan, the question has often been raised whether or not the idea of a geographical evangelistic area is meaningful. There is a tendency to feel that people should be reached in the place where they are working. Nevertheless, it is important for a local church to recognize a certain geographical area for which it has an evangelistic responsibility, along with a responsibility to maintain close relationships with neighboring churches. This does not mean roping off a territory against neighboring churches. It requires, rather, close cooperation and sometimes the establishment of a group ministry.

The Evangelistic Area Plan aims at arousing a church's interest in outreach and stimulates discussion as to what the purpose of the church is in a given community. For this the United Church plans several projects: 1) conducting each year in two districts a concentrated effort to assist the area's own plan of outreach; 2) encouraging pilot projects for developing local Evangelistic Area Plans in rural, urban, and new industrial areas; 3) establishing a long-range plan for starting new churches in "high growth potential" areas; 4) promoting the "house church" movement.

THE ANGLICAN EPISCOPAL CHURCH

The Anglican Episcopal Church in Japan, with 325 congregations, has an ambitious plan for lay training. Three dioceses, Tokyo, Kyoto and Osaka, have drawn up five-year plans for lay training institutes under the leadership of the Japan Institute of Christian Education of St. Paul's (Rikkyō) University. This plan is based on the church's experiences of both success and failure in lay training. It tries to concentrate on the training of the whole congregation rather than on picking a few trainees out of a congregation. To achieve the renewal of the churches, the objective of lay training should be to change the image of the church held by most lay people at present. This objective can be reached, according to the thinking of the Anglican leaders, by a program using human relations training methods in small group situations in which participants can encounter each other in free and thoroughgoing discussion.

Another attempt at the renewal of the church has been a series of discussion meetings in which the bishop of a diocese has brought together vestry members from local churches. In the first few years of holding these meetings, local problems were treated without allowing the attendance of local priests. Now, however, it has developed in such a way that both local priests and lay leaders can participate in the constructive discussion of local problems.

These two projects in the Anglican Episcopal Church in Japan are related to the concept of Mutual Responsibility and Interdependence. As a part of the MRI project of the World Anglican Communion, the Diocese of Tokyo has started an exchange program with the Diocese of Washington, D.C. The program includes: 1) the exchange of visits by bishops of both dioceses; 2) the sending of a missionary priest from Japan and a missionary doctor from Washington for joint work in South America; 3) the exchange visit of thirty high school students during summer vacations; 4) the sending of Dr. Hikaru Yanagihara, a professor of Christian Education at St. Paul's University, to the Department of Christian Education of the Washington diocese for a period of three months.

The Anglican Episcopal Church in Japan is now trying to enlarge its evangelistic efforts, especially in the field of industrial and student evangelism.

THE LUTHERAN CHURCHES

After the end of World War II, most of the churches of Lutheran background withdrew from the Kyōdan. Like other denominational groups that chose the same postwar course, they were confronted immediately with the problem of re-establishing a single church body in terms of the tradition they sought to preserve.

Quite naturally, one of the first steps in this process was the reopening of a theological seminary for the training of pastors. Secondly, they turned to matters of management of the schools previously related to the Lutheran missions, of which the churches themselves were products. Finally, they centered on the fundamental questions of policy and methods in the main business of evangelism.

Before this process had gone very far, the Communist take-over in China forced the Lutheran missions there, along with others, to leave the mainland. As a result, some ten Lutheran mission groups came into Japan. By 1952 the plurality of Lutheran efforts had become enough of a problem to prompt an All-Lutheran Free Conference, to provide a forum for discussion of mutual interests. One central objective was a comity plan, by which Lutheran work would be equitably distributed over the Japanese islands. In the course of conversations, a suggestion was made that the missions unite their work.

Meanwhile, the indigenous churches founded by former Lutheran missionary labors had themselves matured to the point where they could take up the issue of unity. They entered into study of a common constitution, and moved in 1963 to the formation of the Japan Evangelical Lutheran Church, uniting churches related to missions of the American Lutheran Church, the Lutheran Church in America, and of Denmark, Finland and Germany. There are 138 congregations in the Japan Evangelical Lutheran Church.

Churches affiliated with the mission of the Lutheran Church—Missouri Synod were consolidated in the Japan Lutheran Church, and affiliated congregations now number 58. This church later began consultations with the Japan Evangelical Lutheran Church for possible merger, and these discussions are still going on. There is already agreement on exchange of pulpits and sharing in Holy Communion, and a single theological school has been proposed. The latter recommendation, still in the committee stage, is related to yet another possibility, that the Lutheran seminary be moved to a site near the largest theological school of the United Church, Tokyo Union Theological Seminary (adjacent to International Christian University). Studies are in process for a common hymnal and liturgy, as well as a center for evangelism through mass media such as television, radio, films and other audio-visual methods.

A number of Lutheran mission groups have assumed a relation to the Japan Evangelical Lutheran Church similar to the cooperative relationship developed between the Interboard Committee for Christian Work in Japan and the United Church of Christ in Japan. These cooperating groups include the Japan Mission of the American Lutheran Church, the Japan Lutheran Missionaries Association of the Lutheran Church in America, the Lutheran Evangelical Association of Finland, the Danish Missionary Society, the North German Mission and a special United Scandinavian Mission to Buddhists.

Until recently, the Lutheran churches in Japan have primarily emphasized strengthening the church as a whole. Interest is now shifting to the local congregation as the key "fighting unit" on the frontier of evangelism. In the early postwar days of reorganization, the church at large was a natural center of focus; now it is important to see the local church *as church.*

On the other hand, there has also been a tendency for individual pastors to follow their own personal leading in evangelistic strategy. As each congregation discovers its own reality as church, it becomes important to emphasize team-work in a given area, to cooperate in overcoming the isolation and limitations of the local congregations. Consequently, training of pastors for joint action is being given top priority.

Another element in the Lutheran evangelistic thrust derives from evaluation of past attitudes, when efforts were centered in the church programs in the hope that people would be attracted to them and come to church. Now the call is to go out into the community, into society, and so engage with people in their common life that the church becomes meaningful for them. A Central Committee for Long Range Planning has been set up with responsibilities for implementing this program of evangelism.

Several aspects of this projected evangelistic thrust are noteworthy. One is renewed emphasis on Bible study, especially because lay people are to take the initiative and give direction to it. Another is the determination that each layman have a clear grasp of the essential nature and mission of the church. More emphasis is to be put on church music and on lay participation in the worship life of the church.

Statistics for the united Lutheran body for 1965 give a membership of 20,000, a 37 percent increase over 1964.

THE BAPTIST GROUPS

The overriding concern of indigenous Baptist churches and related missions is promotion of the overall strength and evangelism of the church. Emphasis is given to the proper placement of churches and to the actual increase in committed followers. Though there is perhaps less attention given to meeting local community needs or dealing with the nation and culture as a whole, there is a definite zeal for winning persons for Christ.

The Japan Baptist Convention, related to the Southern Baptist Convention in the United States, was also one of the groups that left the United Church in 1947. At that time the Convention claimed only 15 churches. By 1960 its company had grown to some 70 churches, and at that time the Convention embarked on a Five-Year Advance Movement aimed at doubling the strength of its churches. By 1965 it listed some 101 churches and preaching centers, a healthy 25 percent growth during the five-year period. A second Five-Year Advance has been initiated for the years 1966-1970, which is to reach its climax, it is hoped, by the time of the World Baptist Convention in Tokyo, in 1970.

Key steps in the second five-year plan include, first of all, a goal of three new preaching points every year. A central evangelism office has been set up to back this program, and it is expected to provide support sufficient for the erection of a church building and parsonage at each of the points. The plan also calls for the assignment of an experienced pastor to the pioneer projects, instead of the past practice of assigning new graduates from the seminaries.

Another key step in the second Advance period aims at doubling the membership of each existing church. For this, no new methods are envisaged. Rather, it is to be effected through evangelistic witness and education directed through the daily lives of committed church members. Mobilizing women's groups, youth fellowships and related schools and agencies indicates that the spotlight is on existing channels, not ones newly conceived.

A fourth step, and one distinctive of the Baptists' plan, emphasizes the church school programs. The purpose of this step, obvious enough though often overlooked, is improvement at all age levels. Drawing on the resources of an Asia Sunday School Crusade, immediate measures call for the selection of ten pilot churches where model church schools will be developed.

The fifth and final phase of the second Advance program is the retraining of the church's own ministers. The pastors, like their colleagues in churches all over the world, have become too much engrossed in the routine administrative tasks of their churches, exhausting energies that they could better use as spiritual leaders of their flocks. Renewal of the spiritual leadership role of ministers necessitates, most of all, the revival of the spiritual life of the pastors. It is significant that this emphasis has come from the consciousness of the pastors themselves.

The Japan Baptist Union embraces indigenous churches growing out of the efforts of the American Baptist Foreign Mission Society. In 1964 there were 40 related churches and preaching centers. The early policies of missionaries of this group, who arrived in the 1870's, focused on strategic planting of churches and on publication of biblical and other Christian literature. In time their work included the establishment of schools and social welfare agencies. At a fairly early stage a comity agreement was reached with the "Southern" Baptists, who assumed responsibility for the large southern island of Kyushu, while the "Northern" Baptists directed their efforts to the northeastern, central and western (Tohoku, Kanto and Kansai) districts of the main island of Honshu. An important motivation in this early period was to reach places otherwise untouched, to go where no one else had gone.

Over a period of time following World War II, most of the congregations historically related to the American Baptist Foreign Missionary Society withdrew from the United Church, although several substantial congregations remained. In 1958 the congregations outside the United Church formed the Japan Baptist Union. One of their leaders sees their work as complete devotion to personal evangelism, even in schools and related agencies. While the Baptist tradition involves a congregational system and, thus, should issue in considerable lay activity, the strong tendency has been toward pastor-centered churches—a trait common to almost all Christian groups in Japan. Even though the weight of leadership is overwhelmingly on the side of the pastors, the basic intention is, of course, the strengthening of each local church.

Compared to other Baptist groups in Japan, the Union is greatly advanced in its indigenous leadership. The appointment of foreign missionaries, for instance, is handled within the responsible councils of the national church.

The Japan Baptist Union also has a five-year approach, having begun its second five-year program in 1965. It is structured around four main points: programs to strengthen the local churches, pioneer evangelism projects aimed at self-support, development and promotion of special forms of ministry and promotion of church unity. Since the first five-year program produced seven new churches, two of which are already self-supporting, a similar effectiveness is hoped for in the second five-year program.

There are a number of other smaller Baptist mission groups, some of which are associated with the Japan Baptist Alliance. Not a few Baptists are active in independent missions, but limitations of space prevent a fuller treatment of the various groups.

THE PRESBYTERIAN GROUPS

Most congregations of Presbyterian lineage remained within the United Church of Christ in Japan. Their relations go back to the former Presbyterian and Reformed Church of Japan ("Old" Nihon Kirisuto Kyōkai). Presbyterian and Reformed churches that did not remain in the United Church comprise what is known as the Church of Christ in Japan ("New" Nihon Kirisuto Kyōkai), with 87 churches and 21 preaching centers.

An additional grouping of Presbyterian and Reformed churches formed after World War II makes up the Reformed Church in Japan (Nihon Kaikakuha Kyōkai), with 32 organized churches and 30 preaching centers.

The Church of Christ in Japan places a strong emphasis on doctrine and pays less attention to practical activities.

Like most other groups, though, it seeks the necessary strengthening of the life and witness of its own local churches.

A matter of growing interest is the Centennial of the Presbyterian and Reformed Churches, which will take place in 1972. One of the important factors being emphasized in the time before the Centennial is the reshaping of theological education. An important measure calls for students to receive a four-year college education before entering theological school. While this church also aims toward self-support, it seeks to achieve this aim without hampering the needs of evangelism in its ongoing program.

The Church of Christ is not yet a member of the National Christian Council of Japan, for it feels that the latter's inclusion of nonchurch Christian agencies weakens its structure as a possible council of *churches*. Nonetheless, this church is seeking fellowship with the World Council of Churches, and thus with churches around the world, and the prospects are that it will eventually accept affiliation with the Japan National Christian Council.

The Japan Mission of the Presbyterian Church in the United States ("Southern") has a valuable historical relationship with the Church of Christ and also with the Reformed Church. In the postwar years, however, many missionaries of this mission have elected, in accordance with the freedom granted in the constitution of the mission, to affiliate with the United Church of Christ in Japan (Kyō-dan). The Presbyterian Church in the United States is now officially related to the United Church through the Interboard Committee channels.

OTHER PROTESTANT GROUPS

There are some 109 varieties of Christian mission groups in Japan, the majority of Protestant or evangelical orientation. Apart from the large Protestant church organizations already described, most of the remaining groups have "conservative" tendencies and are relatively small. The majority come from North America, though European, New Zealand and Australian groups are included in the larger figure.

The more established Protestant groups tend to turn over leadership to indigenous leaders, but most of the "mission" groups operate independently. Acting from relatively limited bases, they naturally focus primarily upon increasing the numbers of those who accept Christ.

Among these groups are the Pentecostal missions. Their work has experienced remarkable growth in numbers, with special emphasis on bringing families into fellowship.

The Seventh-Day Adventists have provided the wider Christian movement with excellent work in the field of medicine, in addition to their evangelistic efforts. The Salvation Army has a strong record of social welfare work. The Society of Friends has carried forth its concern for peace and anti-nuclear programs, and has labored diligently for reconciliation between Japan and its nearest neighbor, Korea.

An interesting Christian body, native to Japan, is the Church of the Spirit of Jesus. It is noted for sending Japanese missionaries to Brazil, Argentina, Taiwan, Hawaii and California, as well as to Korea. It works, initially at least, with Japanese people living abroad—a ministry, as it were, to the Japanese "diaspora" throughout the world.

THE NON-CHURCH MOVEMENT

The picture would hardly be complete without mention-
ing the many spontaneously organized, lay-directed, informal
groups that meet throughout the country for Bible study,
fellowship and occasional service to their fellowman. One
of these is the Non-Church movement, a phenomenon
unique to Japan. Because this movement is not institutionalized, and thus produces no statistical records, it is extremely difficult to grasp its intent and to measure its effect.
Its character, however, is not quite so elusive.

Essentially it is a lay movement, with innumerable groups,
each centering around its own leader. They meet in homes,
schools, hospitals—in any and all kinds of places. The different groups are bound together in fellowship by occasional large rallies and the distributed literature of the movement. This literature ranges from simple mimeographed
sheets to books written by the more widely recognized
leaders. A group can emerge wherever someone takes the
initiative to start one; and it can die out just as easily when
the leader passes from the scene.

While an accurate estimate of the numbers involved is
almost impossible to make, the movement is estimated to
have from twenty to fifty thousand members. (This estimate, however, overlaps with the registered membership of
many churches.)

In small cities and towns the groups flourish, though their
popularity may well be caused by the relative absence of
other alternatives for Christian study and fellowship. Among
large city groups it is increasingly the pattern to hold Christ-

mas and Easter rallies on a large scale. On such occasions the expenses for a rented hall are borne by those attending, and no organization or bookkeeping is necessary. Neither are there pastors, officers or other institutional means for conducting regular meetings.

On the other hand, the regular meetings are quite similar to simple worship services held in most other Protestant churches in Japan. The Bible, hymnal and corporate prayer are as central to fellowship as they are in the established churches.

Professor Goro Maeda of Tokyo University, for example, has been holding meetings every Sunday for the past thirty years, using the music room of a private school, offered by the owner of the school free of charge. There are no special publicity measures aside from word of mouth of the regular participants to their acquaintances.

The primary interest among the Non-Church groups is Bible study. Hymns are sung and prayers are offered, following which the leader gives an exposition of the Bible lesson. Within the groups, the fellowship relation is strong.

The term "Non-Church" includes even those who read and study the Bible individually, for instance, a person in a hospital bed or a remote country village. It is sometimes said that they are the *true* Non-Church. Such persons receive encouragement, of course, from the distributed literature of the movement.

A missionary related to the United Church, who was formerly assigned to the sparsely populated northeastern region, reports meeting once with an elderly gentleman farmer who engaged in individual Bible study. This old farmer had been

accosted by a radically conservative missionary who was passing out tracts that presented a peculiar interpretation of the
New Testament. Because the old man, in the seriousness of
his study, had taught himself Greek in order to read the
New Testament in the original, he recognized the peculiari-
ties of the tracts immediately. Such an experience witnesses
to the vitality of a movement which claims as its founder
the venerable Kanzō Uchimura.

THE ROMAN CATHOLIC CHURCH

The history of Catholic missions goes back to 1549, when
the first Jesuit missionaries reached Japan. Their early suc-
cesses were soon cut off by the isolation policies of the
Tokugawa government, put forth from 1638. The Roman
Catholic Church renewed its work in Japan soon after the
country was opened up in the latter half of the nineteenth
century, and has strengthened its position to the point that
its membership is only slightly less than the total number of
Protestants.

Today, however, the Roman Catholic Church faces a turning point in its life and mission in Japan, as it seeks to carry
out the new emphases issuing from the Second Vatican
Council. These changes will be carried out slowly, to be
sure, yet it is possible to discern a number of new directions.

One of these, quite naturally, is the shift from the exclu-
sive use of Latin to a more extensive use of the Japanese
language in worship. Innovations in the use of the vernacular
in Catholic liturgy in Japan were made first on March 7,
1965. A well-planned schedule calls for selective and gradual
replacement of Latin terms by Japanese equivalents, and

careful study and preparation are being made for each change.

An element of special interest is the increased conversation with major Protestant bodies, especially in the fields of university evangelism and cultural studies relevant to general and special evangelism. Although plans are still in a stage of preliminary consideration, there is a mutual desire among Protestants and Catholics to have a common translation of the Bible in the Japanese language.

The search for renewal within the Roman Catholic Church has brought various groups into greater dialogue with each other. Such dialogue involves different religious orders, different age groups, and various social and regional groupings, all in an attempt to overcome what has been called by one leading figure "poor circulation of the life-blood of the church."

Catholics in Japan, like those in Europe and America, have turned their attention anew to the importance of the laity in the life of the church. They aim to lessen the over-emphasis on the priestly role, believing that the layman has a meaningful role in his own right. A program of lay training is being initiated, planned by laymen with priests acting only as advisers. The central content of this program focuses on the meaning of the gospel itself, as the point from which renewal of the laity and of the church begins. Another expression of lay emphasis is the Catholic Association of College Graduates, which encourages lay witness in daily life, especially in social, economic and political institutions.

As in a number of Protestant bodies, attention is given to

retraining priests and to revamping the theological education program. The present curriculum has been assessed as too theoretical and too structured for lively response to real-life issues, and therefore revisions are aimed at personal involvement of seminarians in the content of their studies. Roman theological students receive three years' training in philosophy and other subjects before going on to four years of theological work. Heretofore, the first year of theological study included a course in basic theology, which presented an apologetic understanding of divine revelation and provided the doctrinal frame of reference for all theological study leading to graduation. Now, this course is to be placed at the end of the theological curriculum, as the climax toward which the student works. It will serve to organize his years of study, rather than to direct them.

No biblical studies have been included previously in the philosophy course, but now they will be, in order to familiarize the student with this perspective so that he can hold it in tension with other studies. This innovation is in line with the intention to correlate theological study more fully with cultural studies.

To bring the whole program into fuller encounter with the workaday world, students are to be released for a full year after completion of the three-year philosophy course. During this time they will take a secular job, reflect on their study and evaluate their decision and motivation in continuing the theological program and preparation for the priesthood. In other words, the goal is to draw the seminary life closer to the common life of the people of the church and to the culture of Japan.

In evangelism Roman Catholics have sensed that they, much like the Protestants, have too often sat in the churches and waited for people to come to them. Here too, then, the cry is to go out and reach the people. A related matter is the self-criticism, especially among younger churchmen, that the church has often acted to ameliorate social problems, but that it has seldom acted to prevent them through aggressive social action.

There is further soul-searching about church development. As in all episcopal structures, much depends on the bishop's policy, and action by the bishop within the institutional framework is often slow. In addition, there is the factor that the bishops represent the indigenous leadership of the Roman Catholic Church in Japan. National churches tend to appear conservative compared, for example, with religious orders of the church, which receive more support from abroad and thus can move with greater flourish. These orders can purchase large lots and build impressive buildings—impressive to Protestants, certainly!—whereas the simpler church buildings of the indigenous body appear meager. Protestant groups also know something of the struggle, which is being carried out by both national clergy and missionaries alike, to prevent the church's appearing too much like a direct importation from the West.

Such tension can appear elsewhere, for instance in the field of publications. The well-functioning orders can put out impressive material, while the indigenous church may still be limited in what it can do. These matters are crucially important to the overall implementation of the Roman Catholic mission in and to Japan. Even so, we must remember that the orders have served to give this church a leading place among the Christian bodies in Japan.

A special word is due to the establishment of the new cathedral in Tokyo, which was dedicated in a special Mass on December 8, 1964. The splendid building, made possible through a generous donation from the Archbishop of Cologne, Germany, was designed by Kenzō Tange, a well-known non-Christian architect. The Roman Catholic authorities felt that his contribution was symbolic, that is, through him and his work the whole Japanese nation was dedicated to the glory of God. Tange also designed the Tokyo Metropolitan office building and the now-famous indoor swimming pool for the Tokyo Olympics.

Christian Schools and Social Welfare Agencies

Primary attention has been given in this chapter to the life and work of the churches, but no picture of the Christian community in Japan would be complete without a word on the church-related schools and social welfare agencies.

Essentially there are two types of Christian schools. One type includes schools with a relatively long history, related to churches with similarly long histories. Having established broad bases of Christian life, they range far beyond narrowly conceived, purely "evangelistic" interests. They seek to address and to serve the culture as a whole, offering substantial programs of education and enjoying a strong reputation as good schools.

The other category includes smaller, newer schools, related to smaller and more recently established churches and missions. They tend to serve more directly the strictly evangelistic drives of their parent bodies. Moreover, whereas the older and more established schools are almost entirely within the domestic economy, seeking overseas aid only for special needs, the younger institutions are supported largely from abroad.

Perhaps unique to the Japanese churches are the multitude of kindergartens, operated by and usually located in or near churches. These provide, in addition to useful service to their communities, a sizable portion of many church budgets. The kindergartens are a wholesome channel for community contacts not otherwise easily gained. Many pastors receive much of their personal support as principals of these preschool programs. From one point of view, they are a real help to churches otherwise unable to be self-supporting. On the other hand, it can be and is argued that they are a burden to the churches, especially the pastor, because so much time must be spent in administration of the kindergarten.

One of the great contributions of the Christian movement has been the providing of education for thousands of children, often within deprived social groups, for example, young girls in the prewar days when facilities were too few and the principle of women's education was not established. The Christian schools today, along with other private schools, are beginning to face a crisis, especially at the junior high level. There has been an overall decrease in children of junior high age, and at the same time the public schools have been increasing their facilities. The public schools are less expensive, so that their student bodies are growing. Many private schools have been forced to close, including some of the Christian schools.

It is difficult for all private schools to keep up with the quality standards of publicly supported institutions. Nowhere is this more painfully felt than at the university level, especially in the fields of natural science and engineering, because of the expensive equipment required. In a country riding the crest of the technological revolution in industry and public life, the Christian schools face an uphill road in competing for the better students and teachers. Nevertheless, remembering the great contributions of the past, many people in the Japanese nation value the role the Christian schools will continue to play in providing able leadership not only for the church but for the nation.

Social service in Japan was started largely by Christian groups. Although the greater share of the welfare work is now being carried by public institutions, Christian agencies still have a unique function in providing dedicated personnel, in experimenting with new methods and in introducing new insights and concerns.

A pressing issue for the entire Christian community as it moves into the second half of the twentieth century is the definition of the proper and necessary character of a truly indigenous church. Indigenization has two dimensions. One is the question of how to sow the seed of the gospel in the soil of Japan's culture. The other is how to cultivate and nurture the native soil itself so that it will receive the seed and bear good fruit. The church in its inner life, the schools and social agencies of the Christian community, have a long and crucial service ahead of them in finding and expressing in the life of Japan the true forms of the Christian faith.

4

CRUCIAL CHALLENGES AND STRATEGIC MINISTRIES

CHARLES H. GERMANY

The wonderful world of children's stories in Japan contains the tale of Urashima Taro. Urashima, a simple fisherman from a seaside village, one day rescued a turtle from a gang of boys and returned it to the sea. Sometime later the turtle transported Urashima to the enthralling palace of the princess at the bottom of the sea.

Urashima stayed to enjoy the enchantment and wonder of this realm only a brief time, or so it seemed, and then asked the princess to return him to his home and loved ones. Deposited by the turtle on the shore near his home, Urashima entered a strange village in which neither "shadow nor shape" of the old remained. Suddenly, Urashima turned into a very old man.

Japan Old and New

I thought of the story of Urashima last year when, after barely a year's absence from Tokyo, I tried to direct a taxi driver to our former home near Shibuya and got lost. The familiar guideposts were gone. Under the pressure of preparation for the Olympic Games, streets had been widened and the lines of shops and stores had new facades. Modernized roadways long under construction in scores of separated areas had suddenly been connected, changing the geometry of the landscape. The reality of "Japan today" emerged with a sudden and sharp clarity.

Instead of a contemporary who has been absent from Japan for only a short time, what if, for example, Ieyasu, who moved the Tokugawa military headquarters to the strategic fishing village of Edo (Old Tokyo) in the sixteenth century, were suddenly to find himself in his *Yoroi* (warrior's armor) on the Ginza! I think he would suddenly feel very old.

But, and here is the provocative thought, if Tokugawa Ieyasu could stand the first shock, and perhaps lean for a moment against the corner of Wako's Department Store and quit staring stupidly at the *Dorimu Tawa* (Dream Tower) across the street, he might begin to collect his shattered wits. After a short time, he would begin to find familiar things in the midst of all that was new. Perhaps he would turn into the Embujo Theater a short distance away and there discover, on the stage of *Kabuki*, Japan as he had known it. Or in some small back street he might follow a familiar cooking smell to a not-too-different table. If he could muster courage to board a bus going to a residential area, it is quite likely that he could push through someone's garden to the back of a house and find familiar architecture. He would see a Japanese businessman who at the close of a day had returned to his hot bath, his *kimono* and his *tatami*. It would be a little different, but familiar. The man's wife might appear somewhat audacious, but still attentive and gracious. The attitude of the teen-age children would puzzle Ieyasu, but by now he would be sufficiently reoriented to face some questions.

Compared with Asia as a whole Japan has attained a phenomenal degree of modernization. But within this radical newness there is a subtle and unmistakable continuity between contemporary Japanese culture and past tradition. As early as 1954, books began to appear emphasizing the "revisionist" tendencies in Japanese society, meaning that the Japanese were exercising an inalienable right to modify changes introduced from the outside in accordance with national integrity. A new day is pushing in, but Japan is adjusting, not capitulating.

Now, against this background, let us turn to the Christian church in Japan. How is the church responding to the new day? Is the church identifying itself primarily with the currents of change, or with the elements of continuity, with tradition?

Let us put it this way. Instead of Ieyasu, suppose Masahisa Uemura, who was introduced in the first chapter, were suddenly to appear to spend a week in a contemporary Protestant church. Uemura, compared with Ieyasu, is a much more modern figure. It was as late as 1873 when young Uemura became a Christian, at the age of seventeen. Still, he was a leader in the early period of the Protestant Christian church in Japan, and it would be interesting to have his commentary on the church today. One has the strong suspicion that

Uemura's first impression, beyond that of a few stylistic changes, would be no more startling than if he had come back to church after only a good night's sleep. The order of worship would be little changed and, depending on the preacher, the sermon would not be unfamiliar. The patterns of fellowship would not make him ill at ease. By and large, the pastoral ministry would not be new.

Uemura would want to linger in the pastor's study, though, because in the books there he would find glimpses of unfamiliar theological developments. Some of the newssheets on the desk would catch his attention. Phrases like *Shokuiki dendō* (industrial-occupational evangelism), *danchi dendō* (high-rise apartment evangelism), *masu kōmi* (mass communications), *goruppu dainamikkusu* (group dynamics) would baffle him. Given his gifts and precision of mind, he would insist on probing the new phrases and the programs to which they are related. As he probed, a new image of Japan would begin to take shape in his mind. He would begin to discover the struggle of the church to develop ministries relevant to and effective in the crucial new developments in the life of contemporary Japan. It is these ministries, in relation to these developments, that we now want to describe.

New Dimensions of Challenge and the Church's Response

This chapter will not try to present a comprehensive picture of what the churches in Japan are doing. It will not even be possible to include all the significant new or emerging ministries. By focusing attention on only five crucial areas of contemporary Japanese life and outlining Christian programs in relation to them, we hope to make clear the character and spirit of the churches today. The five areas to be treated are the industrial world, the urban world, the intellectual-university world, the literature-communications world and dialogue with the secular and non-Christian world.

In thus limiting consideration to five areas, significant matters are being excluded. The most glaring omissions are the rural world and the world of social problems. To exclude the rural changes and challenges is not to say that with urban industrialization these have become insignificant. It is only to say that urban change is the dominant factor in the future of Japanese society. The farming population by 1964 had declined to 24.5 percent of the total population. According to a 1965 Ministry of Agriculture White Paper, the number of farming households depending more on non-agricultural than on agricultural income had by February of that year risen to 41.8 percent of all farming households. The outlook is that fewer people in rural Japan will accomplish more through enlarged or combined land areas and the use of large-sized farm equipment. This situation means that the rural concerns of the churches will be expressed through strategic, qualitative projects. Examples of such projects include Kiyosato Educational Experiment Project related to the Anglican Episcopal Church, the Okunakayama Rural Center related to Japan Church World Service and the Tsurukawa Rural Training Institute related to the United Church of Christ in Japan.

Similarly in social service ministries, one feels that with expanding government activities in social welfare, the Christian social work leaders and institutions will emphasize new pioneering services growing out of Christian concern for unmet, even unperceived, social needs. Emphasis will also be placed on creative participation in secular social services by committed and competent Christian men and women. But choices must be made, and the five "worlds" that follow seem to be the most crucial in character.

THE INDUSTRIAL WORLD

Anyone who has ridden the train between Tokyo and Osaka from time to time during the last few years will probably comment on two things. First, it is now much less of a trip on the new, wide-gauge super express. Second, the most noticeable developments along the way are the new housing projects and the mushrooming industrial plants. Close to fifty large industrial enterprises are underway in Japan today with strong government support. The grandparents, women and children remain on the farms, while industry attracts the men. All this, and more, lies behind the earlier statement that Japan now ranks fourth in industrial output, behind the United States, the U.S.S.R. and West Germany.

Dr. J. Harry Haines tells of a conversation with a Japanese seatmate as their plane neared Tokyo International Airport. The man said, "I have noticed that in the United States as evening approaches you direct floodlights on the steeples and spires of your churches. In England the floodlights shine on monuments of past history. Notice in my country that we spotlight our new industrial plants." In these plants, the Honda motorcycles, transistors and TV sets are produced.

Considering the great human investment in industry—managers, workers and their families—along with the new unknowns, the tensions, anxieties, play of power and dehumanizing forces, what is the church in Japan doing? The possibility that the traditional parish ministry will even come into touch with the human problems of industry is quite remote. According to a survey of the occupational composition of 12 churches with a combined membership of 2,000, reported by Dr. Masao Takenaka, 57 percent of the members were either managers, white collar workers, students or teachers. Only 3 percent were industrial workers. New ministries are demanded of the church.

Postwar beginnings in industrial evangelism. Beyond doubt the greatest impetus toward the development of new industrial ministries in Japan has come through the insistent voices and leadership of a few Japanese and Western colleagues in company with Dr. Henry Jones, a recently retired missionary who served the United Church of Christ in Japan. These men formed the *Shokuiki Dendō* (Occupational Evangelism) Committee of the United Church, and they have campaigned over the course of the past fifteen years for recognition of the critical developments in industrial Japan. The growth of interest has not been limited to the United Church. In strategic areas Lutheran and Anglican Episcopal ministers and laymen have helped organize Christian projects in industrial areas. The Anglican Episcopal Church formed a Commission on Industrial Evangelism in 1963.

Contemporary industrial ministries. A number of encouraging new ministries have emerged from a deepened awareness on the part, if not of whole churches, of active groups within them. In the Harima area southwest of Kobe four churches cooperate in a group ministry that seeks to understand and serve eleven townships. Out of this endeavor came Wako Labor Center in Himeji and the Hyōgō Christian Labor Welfare Center for truck drivers.[1] In Hiroshima a Joint Industrial Mission involves twenty-two Hiroshima Protestant churches. This mission, according to the Rev. Marvin Tack, who was assigned to it by the Japan Evangelical Lutheran Church, seeks to avoid becoming institutionalized and to emphasize involving laymen in industrial mission. Tack concentrates on workers in small struggling subsidiary industries, working through dormitory visits, assistance in the constructive use of leisure time and guidance in self-development. A variety of programs has developed in the city of Toyota, in Yokkaichi, in Kyoto, in Osaka and in the Tokyo-Yokohama area.

Kansai Labor Evangelism Fellowship. The first and most noteworthy project in the Christian ministry in industry is the Kansai Labor Evangelism Fellowship, begun in 1956 by such men as Dr. Masao Takenaka, Dr. Henry Jones and the Rev. Hisashi Mitsui. That year four seminary students from the Dōshisha and from Kwansei Gakuin University's Department of Theology began intern programs under the guidance of the fellowship in nearby shipbuilding, construction and railway industries. In 1958, on graduation from seminary, the Rev. Satoshi Hirata and the Rev. Aimei Kanai became full-time pastors of the fellowship. In subsequent years the fellowship has continued the Students-in-Industry and labor intern programs, in addition to study, research and church leader seminars. Labor unions have turned to the fellowship for guidance in educational, recreational and personnel matters. Kanai, Sato, Miss Michiko Yashiro and others have continued to work closely in personal counseling and advisory relationships with Japan's General Council of Trade Unions, Japanese Trade Union Congress and the Seamen's Union.

Ministers who have come out of the fellowship serve the industrial mission of the church in various parts of Japan. Mr. Hirata spent eight months in India in 1963 as a member of an industrial evangelism team. A second representative of the fellowship is serving in the Coptic Evangelical Church in Egypt, helping to develop a Christian program in industry.

Mr. Mitsui has stated the objectives of the fellowship as follows:

The first is to establish contacts with labor unions and to study those needs and conditions which Christianity may be able to meet. Such a study must lead to concrete action. The second goal is to seek out the Christians involved in union activities, study their problems with them and support their role as Christians in organized labor. Thirdly, we are striving to establish and nurture churches for workers. (*Communicating the Gospel to Organized Labor*)

Nishijin Labor Center: An additional development of outstanding significance is the Nishijin Labor Center.[2] In the northwestern section of the ancient city of Kyoto lies Nishijin (Western Camp), an area in which more than 20,000 workers in the silk-weaving industry are concentrated. Nishijin's silk-weaving industry dates back three hundred years. The industry is not yet modernized and is still conducted on the basis of home or small industry consisting of a few looms. Wages are low and working hours long. Into this area came Mr. Mochinobu Shimo, while he was still a seminary student. He found a number of churches and other Christian organizations, each separately engaged in rather traditional programs. Through Shimo's efforts four churches, the United Church of Christ in Japan, the Episcopal Church, the Church of Jesus Christ and the Evangelical Lutheran Church, together with the YMCA, the YWCA and student groups from Dōshisha University, formed the Nishijin Association. Overseas and ecumenical organizations that have helped in the program are churches in the United States, Switzerland and Germany, the World Council of Churches and the East Asia Christian Conference.

The association's first annual labor school was held in a Buddhist temple. Later Japanese and American Christians made possible the erection of a center building. Here today, a vital program directed by a creative staff is going on in Nishijin. Particularly outstanding leadership is provided by Miss Sachiko Yamane, who was born and reared in Nishijin and came to the staff of the center while she was studying at Kyoto Women's College. The whole range of personal and family needs of the people of Nishijin is the focus of the program. Activities include schools for working people, cooking classes for women, English study, a counseling service, a medical clinic, research activities, children's groups and Bible study classes. The churches, the staff and all voluntary workers are committed to the faith that the redemptive and recreating love of God in Jesus Christ can renew lives and bring hope and joy and meaning to the individuals and families of Nishijin. It is possible to convey the meaning of

Christ for life, the staff of Nishijin feel, when true human communication is established and maintained.

Guiding principles in industrial mission. Some of the principles of Christian mission in industry which the Nishijin Center and the Kansai Labor Evangelism Fellowship have helped to clarify are:

1. Effective service in expanding industrial areas requires the joint effort of churches and Christian groups.

2. The primary and most crucial factor is committed and creative leadership.

3. Industrial mission cannot be content to draw people out of their living situations into centers of worship, study and recreation. It must try to establish and maintain a Christian presence and influence in the social organizations and structures that dominate and determine much of the personal and community life of laboring people.

4. Each person must be helped to an understanding of personal vocation and the possibility that daily vocation can become a channel of service to God and one's fellowman.

5. Christ calls the churches to work for the recovery of freedom and dignity for all men. To answer this call is to share in the ministry which Christ began and which he continues.

THE URBAN WORLD

The *Tōkaidō* (Eastern Sea Way), over which samurai warrior parties moved and along which Hiroshige passed, stopping from time to time to paint his well-known "Fifty-three Stages," is Japan's most famous length of road. For the samurai it linked Tokyo and Kyoto, passing through occasional towns. Today the urban centers along the way are expanding. Tomorrow the Tōkaidō may well be "main street" of a "strip city" 321 miles long.

The rural population of Japan is now less than one-fourth of the urban population. In 1960, 18.9 percent of the total population of Japan was located in seven cities—Tokyo, Osaka, Nagoya, Yokohama, Kyoto, Kobe and Kita-Kyushu. By 1965 this figure had reached 20 percent. A recent government publication, according to the *Asahi* newspaper, predicts that by 1985, 90 percent of Japan's population will be concentrated in cities.

Cities without histories. The amazing new urban phenomenom in Japan is the appearance of a series of *cities without histories.* These cities are on the drawing boards of city planners one year and are taking shape on the landscape a year or two later. They consist mostly of high-rise apartment blocks called *danchi.* An inside headline (it did not even make the first page) in the *Japan Times* early in 1966 read, "World's Largest 'New Town' Slated."

The world's largest "new town," accommodating 300,000 people will be built in eight years on Tama hills in Tokyo's western suburbs with construction work beginning this year. . . . Plans call for the construction of three new universities in the town and a high-speed railway system which will connect the town with downtown Tokyo in half an hour. . . . Besides the three universities, five high schools will be built along with three large hospitals and amusement facilities, including movie theaters and playgrounds. . . .

Japan's largest housing project at present is on the Senri hills in the suburbs of Osaka. 150,000 people live in the development, which covers an area of 2,875 acres. Though sometimes lesser projects are sponsored by private corporation capital, such mammoth developments are usually built and financed by the government-supported Japan Housing Corporation.

The new cities are one serious effort to cope with increasingly crowded conditions. In the present cities, utilities are overtaxed, space averages approximately eighteen square feet per person, traffic is a nightmare, smog is terrible, sanitary services are inadequate, schools arc overcrowded and water is often scarce.

Who peoples the cities? The cities of Japan follow the pattern of cities everywhere. They are the centers of power—financial, industrial, academic, organizational and political. The fine arts find their fullest expression there. The cities are usually the goal for rural young people, particularly for the talented, who are most needed to serve rural society. Hundreds of thousands are attracted by the expanding industries in or near the cities.

Let us now respond to the question, "Who peoples the cities?" on a deeper level. A phrase often used in Asia is the "forgotten peasant." The forgotten peasant is not the farmer tilling the soil, whom the world has bypassed. The forgotten peasant is the rural immigrant to Asia's cities. Rural people in Japan justifiably would not react happily to the term "peasant," but vast numbers of people in Japan's cities are uprooted rural people, enveloped in anonymity. We have been reminded that the anonymity of secular city life can serve the useful function of creating the possibility of individual privacy and freedom in crowded city conditions. On the other hand, to the lonely, confused rural immigrant, anonymity can be destructive. Cities are peopled by many such persons.

The cities of Japan are peopled by men and women whose social patterns, religious customs, value structures and family ties have been disrupted. Family stability has been eroded. Often both mother and father work, so that the *Kagik-ko* ("key children"), the kindergarten and early grade children with apartment keys on strings around their necks, have become a part of apartment block life. Juvenile gangs are developing, and crime is rising.

What are the churches doing? The Keiyo Cultural Foundation is an example. Across the bay from the city of Tokyo lies the Keiyo area of Chiba Prefecture. Here land is being reclaimed from the sea to accommodate new factories and housing. Tatsumi, the first housing project, is partially complete, and now over 7,500 people live there. When complete, Tatsumi will house 25,000 people in 7,200 apartments.

The Rev. Minoru Ishimaru of the United Church of Christ in Japan traveled to the Keiyo area again and again to survey the development at an early stage. He tried to imagine what the new "community," if such a word applies, would be like. Recognizing the need to secure land for a church at an early stage, Mr. Ishimaru reported to the United Church. With the church's aid an acre of ground was secured in the heart of the apartment block area. A temporary building has been erected which serves many purposes— day school, meeting hall, Sunday school, church and pastor's residence. Construction has now started on the first stage of a Christian community center. Because of the projected future developments like Tatsumi in other parts of the Keiyo area, Mr. Ishimaru looks ahead to the need for other Christian centers. The Keiyo Cultural Foundation has been formed to secure funds and direct the building of other centers.

Pastors and staffs of gifted and dedicated people will come, as Mr. Ishimaru has come, to live in the apartment cities. They will seek to learn and to help the people around them see the needs of their community and to organize for meeting the needs. "The servant church," existing within the impersonal, dehumanizing atmosphere of large industrial housing centers, will thus call people to the humanity and fellowship given in Jesus Christ. He is offered as the Lord who not only makes all things new, but who serves in the newness of all things.

The largest "new town" in Japan today is near Osaka, built in the Senri hills. Called Senri New Town, it houses 150,000 people. While he was associated with a church development project near Senri, missionary J. Lawrence Driskill of the United Church of Christ in Japan caught a sense of the challenge to the church presented by the Senri project. During the past three years Mr. Driskill has taken every opportunity to interpret his developing conception of mission in Senri to colleagues in Japan and to Western mission boards related to the United Church through the Interboard Committee for Christian Work in Japan. His vision has been communicated. This spring, the Rev. Toru Hashimoto joined Mr. Driskill in the development of a Christian mission in Senri New Town. Osaka prefectural authorities have accepted an application for land in the new town. Following months of careful survey, study, discussion and prayer, a plan has been prepared. Mr. Driskill writes:

Basically, the plan assumes that our witness must include the two chief elements of evangelism and Christian service to be a healthy project in this new situation. . . . The Prefecture is chiefly concerned with nursery schools to take care of nursing babies so that young mothers from the high apartments can work to help meet the family budget. Also, they are concerned that social welfare provision be made to supervise the *kagik-ko*, the "key children" who let themselves into empty apartments when they come home and are without supervision. With our own concern for evangelism and service plus the Prefecture's appeal, we have developed a Christian Center proposal, including the three elements of a nursery school, a chapel and a child welfare program.

The plans and activities underway at Tatsumi and Senri will indicate the effort of the church to develop relevant new ministries for the great urban growth in Japan. The churches must guard against bringing merely traditional programs to the new urban areas.

As yet an unanswered question is how the churches can unite their resources for ministry in and to Japan's new cities. In Senri, the Lutheran, Baptist and Anglican Episcopal Churches are beginning programs, along with conservative-evangelical groups. Efforts have been made to avoid geographical overlap—but will they be sufficient? The answer, of course, is no; but the positive way toward joint action in the overwhelming new urban developments is not yet clear. Western churches, which gave Japan her denominations, may well remain sensitive to opportunities for encouraging the search for joint action in mission in Japan's cities.

THE UNIVERSITY WORLD

The Japan Information Service of the Consulate General of Japan in New York City reported in January 1966 that Japan's Ministry of Education has approved an increase of 12,660 students to be admitted to the almost 600 public and private universities and junior colleges this spring. An expansion of student capacity by 14,246 had previously been approved by the ministry's Council to Study University Establishment. Thus, 26,906 new places will be open. It is expected, the report continued, that college applicants this spring will number 618,000, against 472,000 in 1965. According to the Ministry of Education's 1964 white paper, "Higher Education in Postwar Japan," the percentage of high school graduates who enter college had risen by 1963 to 28.1 percent.

The leading Christian universities expect that 6 to 10 students will take the entrance examinations for each single opening. Higher education in Japan depends on private institutions to enroll 70 percent of all college and university students.

As of 1964, among the 416 private institutions there were 38 Christian junior colleges, 24 Christian colleges and 9 postgraduate Christian universities. These figures include only institutions related to the Education Association of Christian Schools. Some Christian institutions, particularly a large number of junior colleges, are not related to the association. The long histories of the Christian schools are noteworthy. Institutions such as Dōshisha, Meiji Gakuin and Aoyama Gakuin are only a decade away from a century of existence. Through the years Christian contributions to education at all levels have been significant.

A *new day in the university world*. Though students have played vocal and influential roles in the past in Japan, the atmosphere in the university world today is distinctively new. First of all, there is a sharpened sense of the effectiveness of a corporate voice of protest and resistance. The role of student protest was crucial in the toppling of the Kishi cabinet following the renewal of the Japan-United States Mutual Security Treaty in 1960. Students were active in opposing former President Eisenhower's visit to Japan in 1960. The voice of student protest has been strong in opposing the docking of United States nuclear powered submarines and the signing of the treaty normalizing relations between Japan and the Republic of Korea.

Second, it is clearer than ever before that the impact of secular civilization, with its international character, will be felt particularly in the university world. The concerns of natural science, of political and social issues, pervade the university campus, classrooms and dormitories. Japan's nuclear reactors are located in or near universities. The interest in national cultural identity and international responsibility is a particular issue of university and intellectual life.

Third, the new Japan will not merely evolve. National development will be directed in part along lines adopted through analysis, reflection and interpretation, supplied largely by the intellectual and university world.

The university world—arena of scholarship and intellectual vitality—constitutes a strategic challenge. This challenge is not new in Japan, as Christian leaders saw a hundred years ago, but today accelerated developments suggest that the student-university community should be given a high priority.

Outstanding Christian developments. To summarize developments in the Christian universities and in student centers and ministries across Japan would require more space than is available. Such a summary would include a creative and provocative seminar program at the Student Christian Fellowship Center in Tokyo related to the United Church of Christ in Japan, in which Christian leaders, professors and students are attempting to understand the relationship of natural science and faith in contemporary Japan. It would include a review of *Cassiciacum '65*, an interesting and effective two-day retreat bringing together university teachers with a renowned cultural attaché and churchman of the British Embassy for a "Socratic-style dialogue," sponsored by the Anglican Episcopal Hokkaido University Center. The summary would present an account of the involvement of students in Christian outreach projects around the city of Sendai, conducted by the Sendai Student Center related to the United Church. The summary would include a description of the "process" through which students and student leaders are working, trying to define the role and relationship of Christian students in and to dynamic issues and activities (demonstrations, protest marches, strikes) in the university and politicosocial world in Japan today.

Four such developments deserve particular attention:

1. International Christian University has begun its second decade with a notable first in Japan's university world—the opening of a graduate Department of Public Administration.

Someday, mayors of cities and heads of government bureaus may look back to a conscious preparation for leadership and responsibility carried out at International Christian University.

A further program conducted at International Christian University, which may have wide significance, is a study in values and formation of value standards conducted until 1966 by Professor Maurice Troyer and continued by the university. Obviously, in a day when major attention in national life is given to the absence of an ethical-moral system in education and in life, the International Christian University's values study could have very great influence.

2. A program of special interest is the "Sensitivity Training Program," sponsored by the Japan Institute on Christian Education at St. Paul's (Anglican Episcopal) University (Rikkyō) in Tokyo. The program is directed primarily toward the life and leadership of the church in Japan. Begun eight years ago as a "church life laboratory," the program is an outgrowth of the group dynamics movement and seeks to provide a situation in which participants can come to understand themselves better as they relate to others and participate in group life. A ten-day group "laboratory" program is the first step; and 274 pastors and laymen from a number of denominations have completed this step. Increasingly, "graduates" are challenged to make use of their insights and experiences in their local situations. In one Tokyo church, vital group relations within the church have led to a redefinition of the total responsibility of the church in an important ward of the city, and laymen are active as never before.

3. The Institutes for the Study of Christianity and Cul-

ture developed at International Christian University and at Kwansei Gakuin University near Kobe deserve special notice. Within an atmosphere of modernization, internationalization, and perhaps Westernization, what can and should "Christianization" mean? How can Christianity remain open to creative cultural encounter? Professor Kiyoko Cho of International Christian University defines the objectives of ICU's Institute as the search for the meaning of the gospel in the context of cultural reality, or the effort to relate the gospel and the human situation in the dynamic reality of Asian culture rather than in theoretical or abstract terms. The endeavor may lead, Professor Cho hopes, "to the healthy indigenization of Christianity in the Asian heart."

4. In recent years there has been an effort, growing out of the Life and Mission of the Church Studies of the World Student Christian Federation, to unify or correlate student work among Christian organizations, including churches, the YMCA and the YWCA. The National Christian Council in Japan has supported this effort, and a greater correlation of aims and objectives and the uniting of resources have proved possible. In line with the appointment of an outstanding Asian Christian to the staff of the World Student Christian Federation for work in the Asian university world, plans for new steps in leadership are being studied in Japan. This program will also be related to the East Asia Christian Conference.

Roman Catholic activities. Sophia University (Jochi Daigaku), a Roman Catholic university in Tokyo, is outstanding in its contribution to the intellectual-university world. There are presently, according to Father Joseph Spae,

director of the Oriens Institute for Religious Research, seventeen applicants for each admission. Particularly at the point
of the relationship of Christianity and Japanese culture, the
program of Sophia deserves special mention.

THE LITERATURE-COMMUNICATIONS WORLD

Approximately 99 percent of the population of Japan can
read and write. According to a report in 1962 by the
Mainichi newspaper, 72.1 percent of the adult population
(over 16 years of age) read books and magazines. Because
Japan has only 648 public libraries, readers usually buy their
books. In 1964, 32,229 titles sold 342,790,000 volumes, costing
$356,667,000. The total daily newspaper circulation is ap-
proximately one newspaper to every two people.

A new Christian publishing venture.[3] Christian publishing
began in Japan in 1888, with Japanese laymen at the center
of the activity. In 1943, the ten leading Christian publishers
were forced by the government to merge into the Protestant
Publishing Company (*Shinkyō Shuppan Sha*). There was
little activity until 1946, when a publishing boom began and
a Christian Publishers Association was formed. New bookstores were opened. The National Council formed a Literature Activities Department. In 1964 two hundred Christian
titles sold 700,000 volumes, at a cost of $972,000.

By 1964, according to a Tokyo special committee study,
Christian publishers recognized that Christian literature distribution was disorganized and ineffective and that it reached
only a limited circle of interested people within the total
population. Furthermore, Christian bookstores existed in
some of the cities only, and few people ordered by mail.

The Christian Publishers Association authorized a marketing study and learned that 32 percent of all readers bought secular books by browsing in bookstores. It was clear that a way must be found to put Christian books on the shelves of neighborhood bookstores across the country. Yet in non-Christian Japan it was unlikely that retailers would be interested in small Christian publisher relations.

The Christian publishers decided to carry out a pilot project in a central distribution agency in Tokyo, which would serve as a depository for all marketable Christian books. They would approach retailers with the concept of a Christian bookshelf or nook, attractively displaying Christian books, and use advertisements in local newspapers as a supplement.

In January 1966, after six months of the pilot program, in which 735 retail bookshops had cooperated, sales of Christian books had increased as much as 1500 percent! More important, Christian literature was effectively reaching beyond Christian circles into the non-Christian world.

This promising new development involves as a next step the raising of $347,222, half of which will be sought in Japan, to secure land and a building for a wholesale central distribution center. The pilot center is now only temporarily housed. The World Literature and Christian Literature Committee of the National Council of the Churches of Christ in the U.S.A. and the Christian Literature Fund of the World Council of Churches, together with the German Missions Council, are supporting the program.

The growing mass communications challenge. With a multiplicity of radios in most Japanese homes and a television set in 90 percent of them, mass communications is a multimillion dollar business. The Christian church is still using the media of radio to only a limited extent and television hardly at all. Part of the problem is expense, which limits participation on a wide scale by most churches, and the churches have not yet found sufficiently satisfactory ways of joint support of radio and television ministries. Radio time costs up to $200 for a one-minute "spot" broadcast during popular evening hours and $395 for a fifteen-minute period. Television charges for twenty *seconds* of the best time amount to $445 and $1,100 for fifteen minutes.[4] "The Lutheran Hour" continues in its fourteenth year, and the Seventh-Day Adventist "Voice of Prophecy" in its tenth year. In 1964 fifteen Christian groups were buying radio and television time.

In television, the only regular Christian programs are "The Christian Hour," presented bimonthly by the Osaka District of the United Church of Christ in Japan, and two fifteen-minute Sunday morning programs in Tokyo sponsored respectively by the Pacific Broadcasting Company and an independent supporter. The Southern Baptist Church in Japan is experimenting with the use of television as a supplement to evangelism programs.

The United Church of Christ in Japan, in cooperation with the Interboard Committee for Christian Work in Japan, is extending and uniting regional programs toward the goal of national radio coverage under a Joint Broadcasting Committee. It is hoped that other churches will find it possible to enter into the joint program.

Of the regional activities, the Hokkaido Radio Evangelism

and Mass Communications (HOREMCO) project, centering in Sapporo, is pioneering in the direct relating of a broadcasting and correspondence course program to the life of the local congregation. The HOREMCO project involves the cooperation of a wide range of denominational churches in Hokkaido.

In the Christian mass communications world, interest is now focused on the plan prepared by the Audio Visual Activities Commission (AVACO) of the National Christian Council of Japan for a new Christian Mass Communication Center in Tokyo. The center would provide television and radio studio facilities and a training program for Christian mass communication workers from all parts of Asia through the East Asia Christian Conference.

Finally, in conservative-evangelical circles, a program of mass evangelism campaigns and seminars continues to be emphasized. Attention is also being directed toward newspaper evangelism in the form of advertising, called "advangelism."

DIALOGUE WITH THE SECULAR AND NON-CHRISTIAN WORLDS

Nippon Christian Academy. Near the foot of Mt. Hiei just south of the Imperial Detached Palace of Shūgakuin, Kyoto, is found Shūgakuin House, which is also referred to as "House of Dialogue." According to a statement prepared by such leaders of the program as Dr. Keiichirō Shimada, chairman of the academy's planning committee and professor of political science at Dōshisha University, and Dr. Masao Takenaka, director of study for the academy and faculty member of Dōshisha University School of Theology, there are two central program objectives at Shūgakuin House. One is to serve the needs of men in modern society by providing a place of encounter, where people of all walks of life can meet and consider together the issues of contemporary society. A second is to sponsor a new form of lay training, helping laymen themselves to discover what it means to "be" a Christian presence in the secular world of the factory, the office, the place of commerce and the labor union. Conferences are organized, often according to profession—medical doctors, journalists, university teachers, labor-management personnel—in order that people who are involved in similar areas of life can discuss the problems and opportunities they face.

Shūgakuin House is the second such center in Japan. The first is a retreat house near the sea at Ōisō, near Tokyo. Both houses and the programs that center in them have grown out of the influence of the Christian Academy Movement in Germany. The aim of that movement is to bridge the gap between the church and the secular world, or between the Christian community and the human community. During the first five years of the movement in Japan, from 1957 to 1962, more than 16,000 people participated in conferences, seminars and lecture meetings.

Christian interest in meeting the secular world so that the issues of common humanity are faced within the context of faith is growing stronger in the life of the church and in the consciousness of Christian laymen. The self-centered character of the early postwar period when the church was necessarily intent on the stabilizing of its own life is changing. Movements within the life of the church such as the

Nippon Christian Academy have provided a provocative impetus toward change.

Centers for the study of Japanese religions. Centers for the study of religions are helping to enlarge the church's understanding of the situation of all men, outside the community of faith as well as within it. The National Christian Council of Japan sponsors a study center in Kyoto of which Professor Masatoshi Doi is the new director. It will continue the publication in English of *Japanese Religions* but, significantly, will emphasize also the provision of informative studies in Japanese on the nature and activities of Japanese religions. The studies will help guide Christian ministers and laymen in meeting with men of other faiths in Japan.

Perhaps the most challenging and creative forum for the encounter of Christianity and the other faiths in Japan centers in the program of the International Institute for the Study of Religions, developed under the guidance of the late Professor Hideo Kishimoto of Tokyo University and Dr. William Woodward, who recently retired as a missionary of the Interboard Committee for Christian Work in Japan. The quarterly journal that is published by the Institute, *Contemporary Religions in Japan,* is extremely valuable in providing accurate insight into other faiths, presented directly by leaders of the faiths. The program of seminars, lectures and studies conducted by the institute speaks to all faiths, but is certainly making possible meaningful contact between Christian ministers and laymen and persons of Buddhist, Shintō and Islamic faiths.

We will ask nothing more of Tokugawa Ieyasu and his

reaction to contemporary Tokyo. It would be interesting, however, to speculate on Masahisa Uemura's evaluation of the effort of the Christian church to achieve effective new ministries to meet the great, crucial challenges in Japan today. Would he be favorably impressed? Undoubtedly he would. The extent of dedication and mature planning on the part of the churches is impressive. Would he be content? Certainly not. Japanese Christians and leaders are not satisfied.

If Uemura were to question them, Japanese Christians themselves would probably help define problems in the efforts and activities of the churches. It is likely that they would talk over difficulties such as the following: 1) the unwillingness of the denominational churches to cooperate more fully in the face of the magnitude of the crucial challenges; 2) the hesitancy of member churches to empower the National Christian Council of Japan to take aggressive leadership on their behalf; 3) the unwillingness of churches to broaden the concept of the ministry beyond the present parish-pastoral one and to send ordained men into a variety of forms of service without loss of full standing in synods, assemblies and conferences; 4) the inability of the churches thus far fully to release the potential and power of laymen; 5) the need to define, as quickly as possible, effective forms of partnership in mission between mature, self-aware "younger" churches in Japan and overseas Western churches and mission boards. The new period in Japanese Christian history will necessitate multilateral forms of cooperation that will unite foreign missionaries and Japanese colleagues, along with other resources of the Christian world in and outside of Japan, in one common mission in and for Japan today.

Neither ignoring nor minimizing the difficulties, one feels even so that Uemura would turn to the Japanese Christians about him and cry out *"Shikkari!"* (Hold fast!). He would leave filled with a renewed sense both of the greatness of the challenges and of the possibilities of creative Christian response through obedience to the One who himself, in the fulness of time, demonstrated the new and abiding form of the ministry.

5

THE JAPANESE CHRISTIAN COMMUNITY
IN AN INTERNATIONAL AGE

CHARLES H. GERMANY

In the year 1342 Takauji, chief of the Ashikaga rul-
ing clan, was engaged in the construction of the Tenryū
temple. He needed vestments, works of art and special ap-
paratus. To obtain these he opened trade with China. Two
vessels were assigned, and total trade was not to exceed five
hundred *kwan-mon* ($3,700).

In 1965 Japan possessed 10,813,000 gross tons of shipping.
She led the entire world in shipbuilding, and her mercantile
fleet ranked fifth among all nations. Compared with Takauji's $3,700 in imports, during the first half of 1965 Japan's
imports amounted to $4,145,000,000.

Two hundred years ago shipwrecked sailors cast ashore in
Tokugawa Japan were so ill-treated that international resentment was one of the factors that was creating pressure
for the opening of Japan to the world in the mid-1800's.

In 1964, the year of the Olympic Games, 375,000 touring
"foreigners" arrived in Japan by sea and air. Received with

inimitable graciousness, they were introduced to Japan's art, cuisine, theater, temples, shrines, sports, legislative assemblies, schools and homes.

Twenty-one years after the close of World War II, Japan has risen from destruction and desolation to new levels of economic vitality, social development and political significance. Ambassador Akira Matsui recently served as chairman of the United Nations Security Council. Though the offer was not accepted, Japan offered to mediate in the Indonesian-Malaysian difficulties. A Japanese technologist was a member of an international team that surveyed the Mekong River. Japan ranks fifth among the nations giving aid to underdeveloped areas. All but a few of the world's major universities have faculty scholars from Japan, and in fields other than Oriental studies. In 1949 Professor Hideki Yukawa received the Nobel Peace Prize in Physics, and again in 1965 a Japanese professor of physics, Shinichirō Tomonaga, was one of three recipients of the same prize.

Japanese World Consciousness

Japan's contemporary renaissance has a characteristic atmosphere—a pervading international outlook, or world consciousness, within a spirit of growing confidence. The world seems to be confronting Japan with goals to be achieved, tests to be met; challenges against which the national self-consciousness can measure itself.

The role of Canada, de Gaullist France's new assertion of independence and recognition of Red China, the tension between the U.S.S.R. and China, and the breakup of an international Communist front have given Japan what

Takaaki Aikawa has termed an awareness of a multicentered world. In this world Japan is feeling her way. She belongs at present, in spite of closeness to the United States, to no nation or power pattern. That she will carry increasing responsibility, in more than an economic and commercial sense, in the political and cultural spheres is unquestionable.

Within the atmosphere of Japan's national renaissance and world consciousness, an interesting episode took place during 1964 and 1965. The Ikeda cabinet introduced to the nation the challenge of the creation of an "image of the ideal Japanese man." In Japanese life today, in the absence of the traditional Emperor-centered family consciousness of the nation based on Confucian patterns of loyalty, a new national consciousness and self-understanding are being sought. An advisory committee to the Ministry of Education produced a paper on the image of the ideal Japanese man. He was to be, in a particular sense, a man within the contemporary world, a man both national and international. After the publication of the paper, the search for the ideal man largely subsided because of widespread criticism, including that of Christian leaders. Criticism focused on the unnaturalness of trying to draw up blueprints or fashion molds for the Japanese man, as if man could be mass produced. The national humor, which once criticized a large Tokyo evangelistic crusade for trying to create "instant Christians," was now directed at the effort to define the image of the Japanese man for today's nation and world.

Nevertheless, the effort toward national self-understanding continues; and it is closely related to Japan's outreach into the world. Professor Kinhide Mushakōji of Gakushuin

University, who has taught at Princeton and Northwestern Universities, says that Japan has never produced among its leaders in international relations a sense of urbane internationalism. They have always remained under the domination of national consciousness. The peculiar strength of the past in Japan's history could be a weakness in a present and future age of universalization. It could deter Japan, Professor Mushakōji feels, from a full acceptance of responsibility in world affairs.

His judgment appears significant when one remembers that during the time Japan was reopening to the world in the late 1850's, the time of her modern renaissance and industrial revolution, and again during the renewal of national life following World War II, Japan's relation to the world was primarily one of self-building through creative absorption and adaptation. It is interesting, therefore, to hear informed, fully loyal Japanese voices challenging the nation to a new understanding of international responsibility.

Japan's future course in international relations is not yet entirely clear. The nation must decide—in the not-too-distant future—what her relation to mainland China will be, what policies must govern her trade with China and her cultural and political contacts. She must decide what her position regarding defense will be, and this choice must definitely be made by 1970 when the Japan-United States Mutual Security treaty could be abrogated by either country. She must decide on her policy regarding nuclear arms, because her capability for entering the armaments arena is largely complete. She must decide her territorial policies regarding Okinawa and the Kuriles. She must seek to understand how responsibility can be fulfilled in the world, particularly in Asia, with sensitivity toward the memory of World War II in the minds of Asian nations. All these considerations mean that Japan cannot alone define her role in Asia and the world. Her role will be influenced by the attitudes of her fellow Asian states.

It is well, also, for the people of North America to remember that the United States and Canada will help to determine Japan's role. What these countries expect of Japan will make a difference, if not in the long run, certainly in the short run. Again, a reference to Professor Mushakōji is provocative. It is more important to the United States, he feels, for Japan to become a "reliable friend" than an "unreliable ally." [1] Reliable friendship will come, he argues, through the effort to cooperate with Japan in an endeavor to stabilize the situation in Asia and to raise the standards of life though industry and modernization. Such an effort is much more important, he feels, than the unreliable alliance that will result from the United States' use of present influence in Japan to retain her as a foothold in Asia.

Against the background of Japan's new national awareness and world consciousness, what is the place of the Christian community? It is clear from the previous chapter that the church in Japan is wrestling with new forms of the ministry. It is seeking to face up to almost overwhelming challenges in fast-changing cities, industry and society. In view of the magnitude of responsibility and opportunity inside the nation, is there an inclination and energy to look to the world outside Japan? Let us consider four issues or areas in the Christian community in Japan in arriving at an answer:

the understanding and response of the Japanese church in relation to world Christian mission; the role of the church in world peace; the church's interest in ecumenical relations; the gifts that the Japanese Christian community is sending to the world abroad, inside and outside the church.

World Christian Mission

The year 1959 ushered in the second century of Protestant Christianity in Japan. A series of anniversary celebrations was held throughout the Christian community. The National Christian Council ceremonies were significant. Much of the legacy of the century of Protestant Christianity is held within the United Church of Christ in Japan (Kyōdan).

The anniversary ceremony conducted by the United Church was held on November 4. By the time delegates and guests attending the ceremony had taken their seats, the large Tokyo Metropolitan Gymnasium (no church would have held the crowd) was almost filled with people from all parts of Japan and many parts of the world.

Before the program closed, Iwao Niwa (the late General Secretary of the United Church) presented to the assembly a statement expressive of the deep resolve of the United Church as it entered the new century of Protestant Christianity. A central emphasis in the statement read:

We remember that a century ago the Gospel came to us from across the sea. In this second century, we press steadfastly toward more adequate fulfillment of our task in carrying the Gospel to other lands and toward becoming a church that truly bears its share of the universal calling to Christian mission in the world.

It was clear, as the assembly responded to General Secretary Niwa's statement, that he had articulated a shared feeling. Since that time in successive general assemblies the United Church has given the area of world mission greater prominence and priority. The Overseas Evangelism Committee was raised in 1960 to the status of a standing agency responsible to the General Assembly; and in 1964 it was changed in name and character to become the Committee on World Mission.

JAPANESE MISSIONARIES ABROAD

Organizational changes have little meaning unless persons become involved. A Japanese minister in Canada, struggling to learn English, finds himself at the side of a man near suicide and the strength of his faith supports them both through a long night. A Japanese pastor in Germany discovers the pain of "foreignness" in the service of the church in a strange land. A Japanese minister in Thailand allows the water buffalo in the rice fields, as he goes to his church, to remind him that he must discard the erudite teacher's role and preach to the farmers using such down-to-earth images as sticky rice, bananas, the rainy season, fishing, cockfighting, stomachaches, funerals, water buffalo. Presently twenty-nine ministers and laymen—teachers, doctors, nurses—serve in other parts of the world, incarnating the United Church's concern to share in world mission.

Other Japanese churches besides the United Church have similarly been led to an awareness of world mission. A leader of the Anglican Episcopal Church in Japan expressed the belief that the single most significant development in his church in recent times has been the thought and planning stirred up by the concept of Mutual Responsibility and Interdependence. This emphasis was initiated by the Anglican Congress in Toronto in 1965 and has led to much creative planning within Japan. But, he adds, it has also meant a soul searching about the responsibility of Japanese Christians to contribute as well as to receive, and a growth of interest in the exchange of personnel and resources with Brazil, Pakistan, Okinawa and New Guinea.

The Japan Evangelical Lutheran Church inaugurated in 1964 a ten-year plan to send four missionary families to Brazil. A couple from the Japan Baptist Convention are presently finishing study and are assigned to South America. The Japan Alliance Church maintains missionaries in Brazil and is now planning to send workers to Southeast Asia. The Immanuel General Mission Church, the Japan Holiness Church, the Evangelical Free Church of Japan, the Japan Gospel Church and the Japanese Church of the Nazarene all maintain workers overseas. Other Japanese missionaries work overseas with independent status. The YMCA and YWCA maintain fraternal secretaries overseas.

Remarkable work is also being carried out by the Japan Christian Medical Association, an association of Christian doctors and nurses formed officially in 1949, which now has almost 800 members. One of its strongest activities is to help send a medical ministry to other parts of the world. Through the related Japan Overseas Christian Medical Cooperative Service, eight medical workers are now in Indonesia, Okinawa, Taiwan and Nepal. A leprosy center has been built in India with Japanese funds, and the first group of ten doctors,

nurses and pharmacists left for India in 1965. It is noteworthy that, whereas a variety of support patterns prevails
among the missionaries sent by the churches, with Western
churches sharing in the financing of many, the medical personnel are entirely supported by their colleagues in Japan
through the Christian Medical Association.

Against this background of activities in world mission, let
us look briefly at some special considerations.

SERVICE IN SPECIAL MINISTRIES

A number of Japanese overseas workers are fulfilling special ministries in world mission. A Japanese who specialized
in Christian work in industrial society was a member of an
international team that spent eight months in India in 1963
and early 1964, under the auspices of the East Asia Christian
Conference and the Division of World Mission and Evangelism of the World Council of Churches. In 1964 a ministerial
couple with special experience in industrial mission went to
Egypt in response to an invitation from the Coptic Evangelical Church. An agricultural specialist serves on the
faculty of the Allahabad Institute in India. A highly trained
minister-theologian is a member of the faculty of the Thailand Theological Seminary. In 1963 a leader in early-child-
hood education went to Kenya for a year of special district
work. She is now back in Japan, and a number of students
from Africa have come to study with her.

Another special expression of concern for the world mission of the church is the Southeast Asia Christian Rural
Leaders Training Course, carried out during nine months
each year at the Tsurukawa Rural Institute in Japan. Ap-

proximately fifteen to twenty leaders of the rural life of the church throughout Asia come to Japan each year for the program.

SERVICE WITH WESTERN CHURCHES

Some of the overseas workers from Japan have gone, not to traditional "mission field" areas of the world or to special ethnic groups, but to the staffs of established churches in the United States, West Germany and Canada. A deeply moving and theologically sound truth is bound up in this fact: World mission is a two-way street. It is a fullness of fellowship and ministry within the total Body of Christ in the world. From time to time over many years young converts to the faith have come to the Western "Christian" countries from other nations to tell the story of their entrance into faith, and Western people have been at once thrilled, shamed and inspired. Only now, however, with the deepening life of the younger churches in Asia, Africa and Latin America, are we beginning to see the possibility of the full ministry and fellowship of the household of God.

OLD PROBLEMS AND NEW INSIGHTS

It would be superficial not to recognize that there are problems and pain involved in changing concepts, inclinations and sentiments. Asian Christian missionaries are learning the pain of "foreignness" in strange lands, which Western missionaries have known. In receiving "missionaries" from abroad, Western Christian people are being called to a new humility, which is only a preparation for new forms of God's grace and truth. Younger churches are learning about the complex administrative and program problems in responsibly recruiting, training and supporting missionary families. The church in Japan is discovering that she also has the problem of keeping alive and imperative within the church the "far horizon," the "need from afar," which will compete with funds and personnel for "jobs to be done first right at home."

While all this readjustment in both East and West is going on, though, some great Christian insights and experiences are being recorded. A Japanese minister in Hamburg writes that if it is "natural" to be ministered to by a compatriot, the opposite state of being served by a foreigner should be called "unnatural."

From a common sense point of view, the natural is to be preferred to the unnatural. . . . But I believe that it is necessary even for European and American churches . . . to renew their experience of the unnatural state . . . because God uses the one to supplement the other that we may share in the blessings of the gospel.[1]

Another Japanese minister who for three years served on the staff of a church in the United States describes his experience as he gave the meditation and presided at the sacrament of the Lord's Supper.

How can we account for the fact that a Japanese preacher whose father was killed by an American fighter plane eighteen years ago should participate at the same table with a congregation among whom there must have been some whose kinfolk were treated brutally some twenty years ago, except to say that the marvelous miracle has been wrought by him who is our peace, who has made us both one, and who has broken down the dividing wall of hostility.[2]

THE ESSENTIAL "FOREIGNNESS" IN CHRISTIAN FAITH

What does it mean that the churches in Japan feel that God has called them to world mission? Why did General Secretary Niwa feel it necessary to direct his statement to the Centennial Assembly, and why was it supported? What motivates the churches in Japan to send some of their best-trained men to Egypt, to India, to North America? On the surface, is it not ridiculous? Remember, less than one percent of the population of Japan are Christian. Are the Japanese churches trying to assume a stature in the world church out of pride?

Listen to the Rev. Katsumi Yamahata describe his motivation in responding to a call from the United Church to go to Bolivia. He read about the need in the United Church's weekly newspaper, the *Kirisutokyō Shimpō*. Feeling that he could not remain in Japan "snug in his grace," he applied to the United Church. Some negotiating followed. Yamahata described this period:

I spent days in meditation and prayer. I often tried to write my refusal to the Kyōdan (United Church), but each time I felt something burning like fire in the depths of my mind. I could not quench the passion. For nobody can refuse God's plans or deny his call.[3]

From the perspective of the New Testament, Yamahata's action and the world outreach of the Japanese churches are neither ridiculous nor prideful. Must we not recognize that they are expressions of the work of the Holy Spirit in the life of the Christian community in Japan? If this be true, must we not also recognize that the essential character of world mission is not a movement of maturity to immaturity, of opulence to poverty, of cultural advantage to disadvantage? It is obedience to the Holy Spirit wherever he works.

Would it not be sufficient for the younger churches in Japan—situated as they are within the overwhelming atmosphere of the world of unbelief, with all its great opportunity and challenge—simply to be devoted to the tasks around them? Obviously, in Japan the Holy Spirit is not working in such a way, unless the entire mission outreach, including the "fire in the depth of the mind," is false. There seems to be an essential element of the far horizon, the distant need, of the world dimension of the faith, struggling to express itself in the life of every Christian community everywhere. We thus affirm the appropriateness of the world mission outreach of the Japanese church. True, we see that mission against the background of a renaissance in national life and the world consciousness of the Japanese nation as a whole. It seems clear, however, that the world outreach of the church is not simply a reflection of the spirit of the nation and of the times. Rather, it is the expression of obedience to the vital presence of the Spirit of Jesus Christ, who calls his church everywhere to become the instrumentality of his lordship and his servanthood in the world.

The Role of the Japanese Church in World Peace

No single issue so pervades the thoughts and conversation of Japanese people today as does the desire for world peace, particularly for peace within Asia. The word "mood" has come to be used extensively—the concern for peace is a mood, a pervasive atmosphere. The mood has its origin partly in the memory of Hiroshima and Nagasaki, and of the Fukuryū Maru (Lucky Dragon Ship) incident, in which atomic ash fell on a Japanese fisherman and led to his slow death before the eyes of the entire nation, watching through news media and television. The mood has its origin partly in the recognition that the first arena of concentrated action in the event of war between East and West will be the ribbon of islands just off the East Coast of mainland Asia— Japan, Okinawa, Taiwan and the Philippines—where the major United States military bases are located.

What does the peace issue mean within the life of the church in Japan, and what is the church doing about it? It is from the perspective of concern for peace that a significant insight into the world consciousness and world outreach of the church is seen.

VISIT OF JAPAN PEACE TEAM TO VIETNAM

In June 1965, a number of people in the United States received copies of a letter from the Japan Christian Council for Peace in Vietnam. The letter outlined the anxiety of the Japanese Christian community and the nation regarding the situation in Vietnam and United States foreign policy in particular, and the "desire to talk with fellow Christians in the United States." The letter proposed that a team of Japanese Christians come to the United States, "not to stir up any controversies but to pray together, to think together, and, if possible, to act together to restore peace in Vietnam."

The Japan Christian Council for Peace in Vietnam was a newly formed association of Christians concerned with Vietnam, persons who held responsible positions in the

Japanese churches. The council had raised over $8,000 to send the team to the United States.

The members of the proposed team were Dr. Isamu Ōmura, at the time Moderator of the United Church and minister of the Asagaya Church in Tokyo; Professor Yoshiaki Iizaka, teacher of political science at Gakushuin University; the Rev. Sekikazu Nishimura, member of the Japanese House of Representatives and pastor of the Katada Church near Kyoto; Professor Mitsunori Yamaguchi, teacher of political science at Momoyama University; and Mrs. Hatsue Nonomiya, director of the Department for Peace of the Women's Christian Temperance Union in Japan.

The Japan Committee of the Division of Overseas Ministries of the National Council of Churches in the United States expressed willingness, through the National Christian Council of Japan, to arrange the itinerary and entertainment of the Japanese team. The team arrived in New York on July 20, and during approximately a three-week period met with church and government leaders in New York, Philadelphia, Washington, Indianapolis, Chicago, San Francisco and Seattle.

A major motivation of the Japanese team was to share with Christian people in the United States their recollection of suffering inflicted on the Asian mainland by Japanese militarism in the period leading to and during World War II and of the shame and repentance of the Japanese Christian churches that they did not adequately criticize this direction in Japanese national life. The hope was expressed that the Japanese church's reflection on its history might serve to guide the church in the United States. The Japanese ex-

THE JAPANESE CHRISTIAN COMMUNITY

pressed the belief that communism could not be "contained" by military means. They called for the cessation of bombing and challenged the United States to take creative initiative in bringing the war to a close.

It soon became clear that differences in the understanding of the character of the Communist threat in Asia and of the options open to the United States for responsible action made any joint resolution impossible. On their return to Japan, the team expressed appreciation for the reception given them in the United States, indicated the interest with which they learned that there was present in the U.S. a voice of dissent regarding policy in Vietnam, but found it difficult to feel that their journey had had any marked effect on U.S. patterns of thought. Still, as they indicated, the visit should be looked upon as part of a continuing Christian dialogue.

Aside from the outcome of the visit of the Japanese peace team, there are important collateral considerations. First, it is impressive that the Japanese Christian community was willing and able to take an initiative of this character. It was indicative not only of widespread concern but also of vitality within the community and a healthy understanding of the church's responsibility in national and international affairs.

Second, and more significant, the Japanese church in plans for the visit, in its conduct and in reports following return to Japan, consistently placed the visit *within the context of Christian mission*. It is a part of the total mission that churches share with one another, to find ways of speaking to each other in honesty and openness. Moreover, such a relationship is a means for churches to help one another define the role they must fulfill vis-à-vis the nations and governments. Surely, in the contemporary search for an understanding of United States policy toward the People's Republic of China, the words and counsel of the peace team from Japan remain in the minds of the American churchmen who met with the team. It is greatly to be hoped that the churches in the United States and Japan can continue to talk together regarding peace in Vietnam.

A MISSION OF RECONCILIATION TO KOREA

On September 24, 1965 Moderator Isamu Ōmura of the United Church of Christ in Japan boarded a plane at Tokyo International Airport for Seoul, Korea. The burden upon him was heavy. In February an invitation had come from the Presbyterian Church in the Republic of Korea to the United Church to send a fraternal delegate to their forthcoming 50th General Assembly. The United Church decided to send Moderator Ōmura. In the subsequent weeks and months, however, grave issues had developed in the relationship of the two countries. The two governments had forged an unpopular normalization treaty, and anger was strong in Japan. Many felt that United States influence had been unduly applied and that the real U.S. intent, with some degree of Japanese governmental complicity, was to build among Japan, South Korea and Taiwan a triumvirate of anticommunism that would express United States policy. Within both Japan and Korea support and sympathy upheld the hope for a unified Korea. If resentment was strong in Japan, it was stronger in Korea, in the nation and in the churches.

Before his departure Ōmura met with leaders of the United Church and later with leaders of the National Christian Council of Japan. He acknowledged frankly that the continued estrangement of the Christian communities of Korea and Japan, as well as the estrangement of the two nations, at bottom stemmed from the fact that Japan has never adequately expressed repentance and asked forgiveness for the acts of brutality and oppression that the Japanese militarist regime committed during the occupation of Korea and World War II. He said that he was resolved to take to Korea a message of such repentance and apology. The Standing Executive Committee of the United Church and of the Japan National Christian Council commissioned Ōmura to carry out this mission. This was the burden and responsibility that weighed heavily upon him.

On September 25 Moderator Ōmura was given his seat in the General Assembly of the Presbyterian Church in the Republic of Korea. When the question of his speaking arose, opposition was expressed and volatile debate ensued. After three hours of debate, Ōmura was permitted to ascend the podium and to speak.

Ōmura's bearing is dignified, but unostentatious. His voice is soft. Softly, then, and under great strain, on behalf of the large NCC sphere of the Japanese Christian world and in so far as possible on behalf of his nation, Moderator Ōmura spoke. The assembly became tensely quiet, as each word, wrought out of anguish, spoke directly to the common memory of insult, cruelty and resentment.

On this occasion I want first to speak directly of something which for long has burdened my heart. For the many political and human sins and evils which for thirty-six years to the end of World War II were committed against you by the government and people of Japan under the Japanese occupation the Japanese church deeply repents and from her heart apologizes. Especially, for sacrifices required of you through mistaken policies in the administration of education and religion there is no possible excuse. On behalf of the people of my country I beg your forgiveness.[4]

Ōmura spoke of the disintegration of the Japanese militarist state with the end of World War II and of Japan's resolve to join with Asian nations and to work peacefully for the well-being and glory of the people of Asia. He expressed the hope that ties with the Christian people of the Republic of Korea might be deepened and that the churches might share in the concern for Christian unity, finding a common basis for the exchange of ideas, and move ahead together in common mission. "May your church," he said in closing, "truly serve your nation and testify to the mighty acts of Our Lord."

Ōmura ceased speaking, and a brief moment of silence followed. Then the assembly broke into thunderous applause, while tears filled the eyes of this dignified, gifted Japanese Christian of noble birth—who had been born also into the new reality of Christ's humility, love and hope.

Ōmura returned to Japan and reported on his mission. He said that he felt he had come to know for the first time the feeling of the Korean people. He emphasized the Korean church's struggle for relevance in national life. In December 1965, the Committee on World Mission of the United Church met with representatives of the Korean Church in Japan to discuss closer ties of fellowship. In addition, the joint committee voted to request the Executive Committee of the United Church to send letters of invitation to fellowship to the three churches in Korea nearest in background and character to the United Church—the Presbyterian Church of Korea, the Presbyterian Church in the Republic of Korea and the Methodist Church. If these churches respond favorably and all seems in order, the United Church as a next step will send a small deputation to Korea to listen to and seek to understand the Korean churches and to consider with Korean leaders the ways in which God may lead churches in the two nations in common life and mission.

In direct efforts, then, on behalf of world peace and reconciliation we see again that the Japanese church shares in a national concern. It strives not simply to echo national voices and concepts of peace, but rather to direct upon the problems of peace and estrangement the light of Christ, who calls the church to share in his own ministry of reconciliation.

Ecumenical Awareness
in the Japanese Christian Community

We have seen that a growing world consciousness and particularly an Asian consciousness is developing in Japan, simultaneously with a resurgent national consciousness. The two focuses of awareness are not necessarily antithetical. A sense of national identity or nationalism can conceivably strengthen the international role of a nation. There are obviously negative potentials, as imperialist Japan and Nazi Germany demonstrated before and during World War II. The hopeful and positive potential in Japan today, however,

is that the search for the understanding of national identity
is taking place in the context of a sense of international
responsibility.

It would be superficial to say that the church merely re-
flects in its life the atmosphere of society around it. At the
same time, it would be unrealistic to think that the church's
effort to understand its role could be unrelated to or unin-
fluenced by the dominant concerns in national life. In relation to the question of ecumenical awareness, then, let us
ask what the dynamic movements and directions in the life
of the churches seem to be. Are the churches preoccupied
with a developing consciousness of being the church essentially within and for the Japanese nation, or is there an
equal concern for the international Christian community?
Does denominational self-awareness, both nationally and
internationally, dominate? To what extent does an image
of the church, as one body and as the bearer of one mission
in one world, have significance for the churches in Japan?
Is this image of primarily spiritual significance, or does it
stimulate and motivate efforts toward visible church unity?

Evidence is abundant that the Japanese churches are deepening in self-understanding and in endeavor to be relevant
to the issues of national life. The Japanese churches are in
many ways vanguard churches among the so-called "younger
churches," ranging ahead in depth of maturity and conception of mission. Furthermore, in differing degrees and forms
the Japanese churches are aware of and concerned with
issues of worldwide Christianity and the unity of the church.
Let us look briefly at some of the patterns in the ecumenical
awareness of the Christian community in Japan.

WORLD CONFESSIONAL DEVELOPMENTS

Though leaders of world confessional or denominational associations state that such associations are not meant to replace or undercut the participation of related churches in broader forms of ecumenical fellowship, confessional associations do in fact to a greater or lesser degree influence the younger churches. This book is not the place to discuss the pros and cons of world confessional developments. It is enough to recognize that some of the Japanese churches conceive of their regional and world relationships most meaningfully in forms of confessional association. Many, while retaining confessional ties, also desire to maintain active relations with regional and world ecumenical bodies. The Anglican Episcopal Mutual Responsibility and Interdependence (MRI) emphasis, the Lutheran World Federation, the World Presbyterian Alliance and associations among conservative-evangelical churches are channels through which some of the Japanese churches express worldwide interest and responsibility. The Methodist World Council has had less influence in Japan since the formation of the United Church because there has not been a separate related denominational church.

Both the Methodist Council and the World Presbyterian Alliance have extended fraternal invitations to the United Church to participate. However, though ministers of the United Church have attended council and alliance meetings (as individuals, not as representatives of the United Church), the United Church has not affiliated itself with any confessional association. It endeavors, rather, to express world church relationships through the East Asia Christian Conference and the World Council of Churches.

AUTONOMOUS INTERCHURCH RELATIONS

A significant development in Japan is a pattern of interchurch relations in Asia, established thus far between the United Church and the United Church of Christ in Okinawa as well as between the United Church and the Presbyterian Church of Taiwan. This pattern is termed "autonomous," in the sense that the relationships are established without involving Western mission boards or "mother" churches that may have a tie with one or more of the partner churches.

According to this pattern, after sufficient exchange of deputations and correspondence, churches pledge to each other their awareness of common mission in Asia and their desire to exchange personnel and other resources, such as surveys, literature and studies. Finally, the pledge is written into a formal agreement, which is ratified by the highest assemblies of each of the two churches involved. It is apparent that this is not a form of mission board–field relations, but a highly significant joint confession of interdependence. It may well be that the Asian churches in this period of their lives will find the concept of interdependence a more natural expression of their relations with each other in Asia than with larger and wealthier "mother" churches in the West.

REGIONAL ECUMENICAL ACTIVITIES

The first regional ecumenical structure of significance was developed in Asia. It grew out of the desire of Asian churches to find fellowship with each other and to associate themselves for carrying out some activities jointly. First expressed as the Asia Council on Ecumenical Mission, the structure is now well known as the East Asia Christian Conference, of which Dr. Daniel T. Niles of Ceylon is the forceful and able General Secretary. Japanese churches have from the outset taken an active role in the formation of the EACC and have contributed some of the staff leadership.

It was the EACC that sponsored the three "situation conferences" of 1963, in Madras, Singapore and Amagisanso, Japan. These conferences, more than any activity in the post-World War II period, have helped draw the Asian churches into fellowship, and into awareness of the great tasks before them and the need to confront these tasks as nearly as possible together. Joint activities include leadership training, scholarship programs, exchange of personnel, interchurch material aid, youth activities, a program in the university world including one among university professors, broadcasting and audio-visual activities, conferences and study programs.

Churches in other areas, largely following the pattern of the EACC, have sought to accomplish similar objectives— for example, the All-Africa Conference of Churches and the Conference of Churches in the Pacific.

The National Christian Council of Japan, which is active in the East Asia Christian Conference, has also sponsored its own programs of Christian outreach in Asia. In 1964 four Korean laymen were invited to Japan to meet with Japanese laymen, thus inaugurating a program of lay dialogue between the two countries and churches. In 1965 delegates went from Japan to Korea. The National Christian Council sent forty young people to the Asian Youth Assembly held in the Philippines in 1965.

The YMCA and YWCA of Japan are engaged in regional Christian programs, notably in relation to the World Student Christian Federation. A recent change in policies and leadership has been the occasion for the Japan Bible Society to seek to bring into the society a wider participation of conservative-evangelical leadership, as well as to invite closer discussion with Roman Catholic scholars in Bible translation. These steps are domestic ecumenical endeavors, but they will have significance for other parts of Asia. Within conservative Christian circles an Asian Evangelistic Commission, organized in 1964, and the Oriental Evangelical Fellowship are drawing Asian Christians together in joint crusades and conferences.

WORLD COUNCIL OF CHURCHES AND JAPAN

Both the Anglican Episcopal Church in Japan (Nihon Sei Kō Kai) and the United Church are members of the World Council of Churches. A young Japanese layman was elected to the Central Committee of the World Council during the third Assembly at New Delhi. Japanese scholars are members of a number of continuing committees including Studies, Faith and Order, the Theological Education Fund and the Christian Literature Fund. Japanese writers contribute to the journals and studies of the council. A full-time staff member of the World Council's Youth Department in Geneva is presently supplied by Japan, and other Japanese have served on the World Council staff in previous years.

Probably the most promising endeavors during the past decade in the area of Christian unity in Japan have developed in response to World Council activities in faith and order and in Protestant-Roman Catholic dialogue. A book, *Theology of Church Unity: From Montreal to the Vatican,* was published in 1965 by the Japan National Faith and Order Study Group.

PROTESTANT–ROMAN CATHOLIC RELATIONS

During the Week of Prayer for Christian Unity in January 1965, Christian churches in Kobe held their first ecumenical services. Christians attended a series of three services held at an Anglican cathedral, in a Roman Catholic church and at the English speaking Union Church. A new day is dawning in Japan.

In various parts of Japan ecumenical fellowship groups meet for study and prayer. Roman Catholic speakers are being invited to address Protestant assemblies, and Protestant leaders are speaking to Catholics. It was through the initiative of Roman Catholic priests in Japan that Professor Masatoshi Doi, of Dōshisha University, attended the third session of the Vatican Council. The World Council of Churches helped to facilitate his attendance by making him a member of its delegation. Professor Tetsutarō Ariga attended the fourth session as a guest of the Vatican Secretariat for Christian Unity.

Clearly, there is a vital, lively awareness of the Christian church in the world. It is also clear that the issues in ecumenical relations familiar to Christian people in North America and elsewhere in the West are present in Japan.

Are they not issues inherited from the West?—the tension between world Christian concern expressed through world denominational associations versus transdenominational ecumenical relations; the issue of unity in one place versus world confessional identity; and the issue of Christian unity within Japan and within Asia.

The United Church of Christ in Japan is too little known in the Christian world. This is true partly because of the language barrier, which limits communication in both speech and writing. It is also true partly because some have questioned the nature of the formation of the United Church, as being more a union forged through governmental pressure than through responsible theological and biblical preparation. It is worthy of note, however, that the United Church includes in itself a union of more separate churches than any other existing united church in the world. Moreover, the church was formed twenty-five years ago, and during the years since then the Holy Spirit has been working to purge, refine and grant his grace of unity and order to a new expression of Christ's body. If we say this, however, we dare to add a further and provocative question: When, through what means or endeavor and in what form will the Holy Spirit accomplish in Japan the next step in Christian unity? The question is asked out of hope and expectation that God who has begun a good work in Japan will not leave it incomplete.

Gifts to the Christian World from Japan

The gracious art of giving and receiving gifts has been developed in Japan to an exceptional degree. Much gift giving there is done in order to prompt some desired response, and as anyone who has lived in Japan knows, there is no more perplexing cultural adjustment than that of learning to live with and within the *O-rei* (gift-giving) system. Beyond and above the prudential aspect of giving, however, lies the Japanese capacity to give graciously, almost as if the strict Oriental codes that made the expression of care and gratitude unseemly in other ways taught their expression in the tokens and act of giving.

What are the resources of the Japanese Christian community for strengthening and blessing the church?

THEOLOGICAL INSIGHT

A well-known observer spoke in 1965 of the "scandal of dependence" on the part of theological institutions in Southeast Asia on money from Western sources. Is financial dependence really the scandal? Visit the libraries of seminaries in Asia. Note the paucity of books written by teachers and leaders of the church in each place. The shelves are filled with the works of Westerners. One wonders if the greater scandal is not that Western funds support the seminaries, but that Western documents comprise the content of the education.

With one major exception—Japan! Japanese ministers and theologians are writing their own books. There is a wealth of intellectual vitality, hidden from the world by a *kanji* (ideograph) curtain. But breakthroughs are beginning. Professor Kazō Kitamori's *Theology of the Pain of God* has now been translated into English. More will undoubtedly follow, but this work is enough to let the world know that Japan has a theological gift to make.

What should the Christian world expect from indigenous Japanese theologians? Anyone who expects an exotic, unique contribution will for the most part be disappointed. But is an exotic contribution what the Christian world needs from Japanese theology? Is not the great need that Japanese theologians will take their place in the world's theological community to deal with universal theological issues? The Japanese will bring new lights and insights, which will not only be meaningful within Japanese culture but will enrich the total endeavor of Christian theology, to serve the church in its task of faithful and true witness to the gospel.

LEADERSHIP

Already, Japan has given to the world a great gift of trained leadership. A theologian serves in Thailand, an industrial evangelist in Egypt, an agricultural specialist in India, a doctor in Taiwan, a nurse in Nepal, a minister in Canada. Japanese leadership will increasingly make the full dimension of mission in the Body of Christ in the world come alive. Every church everywhere needs both to send and to receive. The churches in the West have for so long been senders that we are almost offended by the thought that we need to be receivers, that a younger church has gifts of leadership to bring to us. But it is so, and we may learn this truth from Japan.

Women will be present in the gift of leadership resources. This reality is part of a hallowed tradition in Japan. Women, both Japanese and foreign, pioneered in many forms of early education, social and prison reform, service to society, the family and the arts. This tradition of leadership continues today. Few contributions of missionary work in Japan have been more significant than its help in revealing the potential of women in the life of the Japanese church and society. The names spring to mind of Hannah Riddell, who led in service to lepers; Kaji Yajima, who fought for legal support of the monogamous family relations; Michi Kawai, leader of the YWCA and educator. Among many contemporaries in the tradition are Mrs. Ochimi Kubushiro, national director of the Women's Christian Temperance Union and champion of crucial social causes; Mrs. Kiyoko Takeda Cho, professor at International Christian University; Dr. Hamako Hirose, educator and president of Hiroshima Women's College; Mrs. Ganjō Kosaka, of Tokyo's family court; the Rev. Tamaki Uemura, pastor and church statesman; and Mrs. Sumiko Tanaka, member of the Upper House of the Diet.

A further service of Japan to the world consists of her leadership training facilities. The language barrier is difficult, but ways are being found to overcome it. We have observed Tsurukawa Rural Institute's training program for rural workers from all over Asia. A Christian teacher in Okinawa is now making preparation to take further training at Seiwa Women's College near Kobe. Two young women from Nairobi in Africa are studying in a school on the coast of the Japan Sea.

Tokyo Union Theological Seminary has just relocated on land secured from Japan's International Christian University; and the Japan Lutheran Seminary has secured adjoining land and will be moving to ICU. Perhaps other seminaries will follow. If so, there will be found the most exciting and capable theological training situation in Asia.

CHRISTIAN ART

Last week a colleague excused himself early from a committee session in New York City, saying he was scheduled to lead the devotional period for his staff. He was asked what he planned to say. "I plan to tell," he replied, "the story of Japan's shoemaker poet." This is the interesting story of gifted Yoshihiko Ujino, who seeks to communicate faith for life through poems scattered about his shop. People pick them up and read them while waiting for shoes to be repaired. Ujino has a large following and gives evenings and free time to teaching and editing a monthly journal of faith through poetry called *Kumo to Mugi* (Clouds and Grain).

During an extended period in 1965 the display cases in the lobby of the Interchurch Center in New York City presented the works of Sadao Watanabe. Watanabe depicts biblical scenes and personalities with block printing.

A group of creative Christian artists in Tokyo have formed what they term the "Group of Seeds" (*Tane no Kai*). Painters, novelists, poets, dramatists and formal dance artists, they have dedicated their art forms to communicating Christian faith in contemporary Japan. It is possible now, for example, to see the Resurrection of Christ and the Conversion of St. Paul presented in Japan's ancient Nō dramatic form. The presentation in classical Japanese dance by Futaba Hanayagi of the Christian hymn, "When Peace like a River. . ." becomes a high moment of beauty and faith. Recently Mrs. Ayako Miura won the attention of the nation through her novel, *The Freezing Point*, which dealt sensitively with the theme of original sin.

REPENTANCE, RECONCILIATION AND RENEWAL

The final gift is sensitive, and one hesitates to speak of it. Given and received confessionally, however, it may be in our time Japan's greatest gift.

Japanese Christians of middle age and older carry a heavy burden of memory. It could be called the memory of retreat from prophecy, and it is a part of the history of World War II. All Japanese Christians occasionally join in a confession of having failed to speak out against the military state when it was coming into being. Some Christians, notably among the holiness groups, did challenge the militarist sect, at the great cost of imprisonment and torture. Many Christians today, however, confess having a part in responsibility for suffering, terror and death in Asia.

In recent years in Japan there has been a struggle to articulate repentance, to perform acts of reconciliation and to witness to God's gift of the grace of forgiveness and renewal. We saw this in Isamu Ōmura's message before the General Assembly of the Presbyterian Church in the Republic of Korea. It can be seen in another man's effort to build a hostel in Tokyo for students from Indonesia. It was demonstrated in New Delhi in 1961 when a Japanese colleague refused to be transferred from an extremely inadequate room because next door was a Filipino. Beside the promise of finding fellowship with one who carried the memory of Bataan, discomfort paled into insignificance.

In the visit to the United States by the Japanese team for peace in Vietnam, a fact of special significance should not be missed. The deepest motivation for sending the team,

Japanese Christians said, was the memory of their failure to perform the prophetic role of critic of the state and the desire to share this memory and confession with American Christians. The nature of political judgments is not the important issue. The important factor was the gift from one church to another of the confession of failure, of guilt, of repentance, of reconciliation and renewal.

This is a fragile and sensitive gift, but one which in a number of ways the Japanese church is imparting to Asia, to the West and to the world. It is a worthwhile gift because it is needed, because every church everywhere is guilty. Surely we who live with Birmingham, Watts, Harlem and Appalachia are guilty. But we may not see our guilt clearly. Can the Japanese church help us to see clearly? If so, theirs is a very great gift indeed. It is the gift of sight when the absence of sight is doubly dangerous because unrecognized; it is the gift of light when the absence of light is twice dangerous because men do not recognize darkness. Such gifts from one church to another in the Body of Christ are rare, but more than anything else they testify to the presence and power of the Christ of the Cross and the Resurrection, in whom all things are become new.

The nation of Japan is going through a crucial time. There is within the nation both a deep search for national self-identity and a desire for Japan to fulfill a responsible international role.

Likewise within the Japanese church a deepening sense of selfhood is set amid a growing world awareness. We see this expressed in a wide variety of ways of participating in the church's world mission. We see it also in the initiative the Japanese churches are taking on behalf of world peace. We see it in patterns of ecumenical awareness and action, regional and worldwide. The Christian community in Japan is filled with a richness of gifts that Japan desires to share with the world, gifts by which the church throughout the world will find its life enriched.

The Japanese church is seeking to understand its life and fulfill its mission both within Japan and within the world in an international age.

CONCLUSION

CHARLES H. GERMANY

Much like the cresting waves in the wood-block prints by Hiroshige, new forces are lashing the shores of Japanese life today. The forces are comprehensive—social, political, economic, cultural, religious. They are exceedingly powerful. They crash against the breakwaters and rush up the shores relentlessly. The stone of the coastline is being worn away in places, reshaped in others, polished in still others. Nevertheless, stone lasts; and in the same way there is a deep-lying continuity in Japanese life and culture, linking contemporary Japan with her national history.

Japan's own history and culture are resources from which the nation today will draw integrating meaning and direction. This is why Jō Niijima, Masahisa Uemura and Toyohiko Kagawa have meaning for Japan today.

The new forces playing on Japanese national life, however, are too powerful, too insistent, for adequate meaning and guidance to come only from Japan's history and continuing culture. The direction ahead for Japan will be determined by some way of relating her history and culture to new forces from the world about her. Hence, the question, "What lies ahead?" is timely and important.

As Japan faces her future, there are some significant matters to be borne in mind by people in the West, particularly North America. One such matter is the importance of Japan's friendship and goodwill. Testifying before the U.S. Senate Foreign Relations Committee, former diplomat George F. Kennan said:

The confidence and the good disposition of the Japanese are the greatest asset we have had—and the greatest asset we could have in East Asia. As the greatest industrial complex in the entire Far East, and the only place where today the sinews of modern war could be produced on a formidable scale, Japan is of vital importance to us and indeed to the prospects generally of peace and stability in East Asia.

On a single day in Tokyo recently a small group of which I was a member visited two leading Japanese educators, an ambassador and a towering figure in Japanese commerce and industry. Each spoke with confidence of the continuing friendship between the United States and Japan and of the essential identity of the self-interest of North America and Japan.

Does not such a relationship call for greater mutual understanding and the development of depth dimensions in friendly relations? If not, the relationship has only political expediency and pragmatic mutual interest to feed upon.

A second matter to remember is that the church in Japan is set within the nation. It has appointed for itself the task, on the one hand, of being relevant to the issues of national life and, on the other, of preserving prophetic responsibility.

Professor Masao Takenaka says three possible roads confront the church in Japan: first, concern for preserving purity of faith can lead the church to withdrawal from the issues of national life, and the end of this road is ghettoism; second, concern for identification of Christian faith with the issues of the nation can lead the church to adaptation, and the end of this road is superficiality; third, the church can seek what he calls a "style of creative minority," in which the church strives to share the burdens of a suffering and seeking nation and, if need be, to fulfill its task by losing its life that Christ may be revealed as Lord among men. Christian people in North America, as they reflect on the minority character of the church in Japan, may well consider ways to respond more fully to the Japanese church's invitation to joint action in special ministries at the crucial cutting edges of mission in Japanese society.

A third matter to bear in mind is that North America, along with the entire West, has customarily been in a "sending" relationship to the East and to Japan. The church in the West has not yet come fully alive to the rich new dimensions of true "interdependence" with churches of former "mission fields." The church in Japan is now in a position to help the "older" churches discover the fullness of life within the Body of Christ, as fine things are not only given but received. A new era of lay interchange has opened. This will include not only a greater variety of missionary vocations but a growing awareness of laymen in secular responsibilities as bearers of Christian mission as they travel between North America and Japan. Interesting special missions will increasingly take place.

A forward look at Christian relations between Japan and North America shows the promise of a new maturity of church-to-church encounter. Probably few great leaders from the church in Asia made a stronger impact on Christian people in North America than Toyohiko Kagawa. He was a rare, gifted person. His influence deepened the social consciousness of the church of the West. Nevertheless Kagawa, exceptional as he was, touched the life of the Western church under the limitations of a former day in church relations between East and West. Today and tomorrow younger Japanese Christians will be more likely to speak with a directness and frankness at times refreshing, at times painful, but always within the bonds of Christian fellowship and responsibility. In turn, they will expect this from Christian people of North America and the West. This new atmosphere of maturity in Christ heralds a new day. Not only are contemporary forces ushering in a new age in ancient Japan. New stirrings within the life of the church hold the promise of a new age in interchurch relations between North America and Japan. It is a very great challenge to be alive to the demands of this new age.

FOOTNOTES

Introduction
1. Kanzō Uchimura, *Zenshu*, XV. Tokyo: Iwanami Shoten, 1933, p. 579.
2. *Ibid.*, p. 599.
3. *Ibid.*, p. 600.

Chapter 3
1. *Japan Christian Yearbook.* Tokyo: Kyo Bun Kan, 1965, Church Statistics Appendix. All the church statistics in this chapter are taken from the same source.

Chapter 4
1. For a description of this interesting project for truckers, see an article by Kyoji Buma in *Japan Christian Quarterly*, January 1965, pp. 35-40.
2. In this description of the Nishijin project, the writer is indebted to the Rev. Robert Fukada, missionary of the United Church of Christ in Japan, now directing the program of field work in the Department of Theology, Dōshisha University. Interested readers are directed to his article in the *International Review of Missions*, April 1965, pp. 173-183.
3. The writer is indebted in this section to the summary by Dr. Henry Bovenkerk, in *Lit-Lit Reporting*, January 1966, of detailed materials prepared by a research committee in Tokyo on Christian literature in Japan, for presentation to the World Council of Churches' Christian Literature Fund.

4. The Rev. Robert Bruns in *Japan Christian Yearbook*. Tokyo: Kyo Bun Kan, 1965, p. 262.

Chapter 5
1. *Japan Christian Quarterly*, July 1964. Tokyo: Kyo Bun Kan, pp. 186-187.
2. *Ibid.*, pp. 180-181.
3. *Ibid.*, pp. 170-171.
4. From the text of Ōmura's statement, *Kirisutokyō Shimpō* (weekly newspaper of the United Church of Christ in Japan), October 2, 1965, p. 3.

BIBLIOGRAPHY

Anesaki, Masaharu, *History of Japanese Religion*. Rutland, Vt.: Charles E. Tuttle Company, 1964.

Blewett, John E., S.J. (ed. and trans.), *Higher Education in Postwar Japan* (Ministry of Education, 1964 White Paper). Tokyo: Sophia University Press, 1965.

Hammer, Raymond. *Japan's Religious Ferment: Christian Presence Amid Faiths Old and New*. New York: Oxford University Press, 1962.

Iglehart, Charles W., *A Century of Protestant Christianity in Japan*. Rutland, Vt.: Charles E. Tuttle Company, 1959.

Kato, Hidetoshi (ed. and trans.), *Japanese Popular Culture*. Rutland, Vt.: Charles E. Tuttle Company, 1958.

National Christian Council of Japan, *Japan Christian Yearbook*. Tokyo: Kyo Bun Kan, published annually.

Offner, Clark B. and Henry Van Straelen, *Modern Japanese Religions*. New York: Twayne Publishers, 1963.

Passin, Herbert (ed.), *The United States and Japan*. Englewood Cliffs, N.J.: Prentice-Hall, Inc., 1966.

Prichard, Marianna and Norman, *Ten Against the Storm*. New York: Friendship Press, 1967 (revised edition).

Reischauer, Edwin O., *Japan, Past and Present*. New York: Alfred A. Knopf, 1964.

Spae, Joseph J., CICM, *Christian Corridors to Japan*. Tokyo: Oriens Institute for Religious Research, 1965.

Takenaka, Masao, *Reconciliation and Renewal in Japan*. New York: Friendship Press, 1967 (revised edition).

ABOUT THE CONTRIBUTORS

CHARLES H. GERMANY

Colorado-born Charles H. Germany has led a cosmopolitan life. Educated at Oklahoma City University (AB), Drew Theological Seminary (BD and MA) and Columbia University (PhD), he served as a missionary in Japan from 1947 to 1964. There, he spent eight years in rural evangelistic work and seven in administrative work, the last three as secretary of interchurch relations for the United Church of Christ in Japan (Kyōdan). During 1964 he served as Acting Geneva Secretary of the Division of World Mission and Evangelism, World Council of Churches. At present he is Executive Secretary for Japan, Okinawa and the Philippines in the World Division of the Board of Missions of The Methodist Church. In 1961 Dr. Germany was one of the four official delegates of the Kyōdan to the third Assembly of the WCC in New Delhi, India. He served as a member of the Executive Committee that planned and directed the Asian Consultation of Methodist Churches, which met in Malaysia, November 1963; and in December of the same year he attended the first assembly of the Commission on World Mission and Evangelism of the WCC in Mexico City. He is the author of one book, *Protestant Theologies in Modern Japan,* and has contributed to the *International Review of Missions.*

JAMES M. PHILLIPS

Professor of church history at Tokyo Union Theological Seminary, James M. Phillips is eminently qualified to write a chapter on the Japanese church's legacy from the past. Born in Pennsylvania, Dr. Phillips was educated at Princeton University (BA, MA and PhD) and Yale Divinity School (BD); and he also studied at Cambridge University. In 1949 Dr. Phillips went to Korea as a missionary of the Board of Foreign Missions of the Presbyterian Church U.S.A., where he served until 1952. He went to Japan in 1958 and, following language study, was invited to take up his present teaching position. He is at present the Commission Correspondent in Japan for the Commission on Ecumenical Mission and Relations (COEMAR) of the United Presbyterian Church and a member of the central committee of the Kyōdan. Dr. Phillips has contributed articles to the *Japan Christian Quarterly*, the *Japan Christian Yearbook*, the *Kirisu-tokyō Shimpō* (Christian Weekly of the Kyōdan) and to such scholarly journals as *Fukuin to Sekai* (Gospel and the World) and *Shingaku* (Theology).

DAVID L. SWAIN

David L. Swain, a missionary of The Methodist Church, serves the United Church of Christ in Japan as co-director of a student center. A North Carolinian by birth, he received his AB from Duke University and his BD from Duke Divinity School and served for two years as drector of the Wesley Foundation at the University of North Carolina. Mr. Swain has served the church in Japan since 1953. He is a member of the Board of Directors of the International Institute for Japan Studies. He translated into English Takeo Yazaki's *The Japanese City: A Sociological Analysis*; and his translation of Yazaki's *Social Change and the City in Japan* is scheduled for publication in 1967. At present, he is engaged in writing Volume I of *Science and Culture in Japan*, in collaboration with Masayoshi

Sugimoto, professor of physics at Kanagawa University in Yokohama. Mr. Swain is a member of the Student Evangelism Committee of the United Church and of the Strategy Committee of the Japan Student Christian Movement.

YOICHIRO SAEKI

Since 1953 Yoichiro Saeki has been associate Minister of the Shinagawa Church of the United Church of Christ in Japan. Born in Tokyo, Mr. Saeki was graduated from Tokyo's First High School, after which he spent three years with the Japanese Army in China. He received his AB degree from Tokyo University and came to the United States to attend McCormick Theological School in Chicago, from which he received a BD with a major in Old Testament. Mr. Saeki is a frequent contributor to *Fukuin to Sekai, Kirisutokyō Shimpō* and other scholarly journals. He is a member of the directing Committee of the United Church's Research Institute on the Mission of the Church. He is a leader in the Japan Institute on Christian Education at St. Paul's University and has led in group sensitivity studies. Mr. Saeki is secretary of the Evangelism Committee of the Kyōdan and chairman of its Missionary Orientation Committee.

Edited by:

Germany, C~

The Response Of The Church
In Changing Japan

Germany, Charles H. - Editor

Paperback- G

DATE	ISSUED TO